Evaluating

Values, Biases, and Practical Wisdom

D1089292

A volume in
Evaluation and Society
Jennifer Greene and Stewart Donaldson, *Series Editors*

Evaluating

Values, Biases, and Practical Wisdom

Ernest R. House

University of Colorado

INFORMATION AGE PUBLISHING, INC.

Charlotte, NC • www.infoagepub.com

Library of Congress Cataloging-in-Publication Data

A CIP record for this book is available from the Library of Congress
http://www.loc.gov

ISBN: 978-1-62396-915-8 (Paperback)
           978-1-62396-916-5 (Hardcover)
           978-1-62396-917-2 (ebook)

Printed in the United States of America

*For Steve Lapan, my old buddy and close colleague
for more than forty years, the funniest man I ever knew—
unfailing in support whenever I needed help in work and in life—
he played a huge role in both—many laughs,
many beers, many tears.*

ERH

Contents

PART **I**

Where Values Come From

PART **II**

Handling Values and Biases in Evaluations

PART **III**

Practical Wisdom in Evaluation

Acknowledgment

This book has been much improved by the substantive editing of Gene V Glass. He challenged me to clarify and rethink some key themes in the book.

Evaluating, page xi
Copyright © 2015 by Information Age Publishing

Introduction

Reframing Evaluation

My purpose in this book is to reframe the way we think about evaluation, which includes reconsidering some key evaluation concepts, such as values, biases, and practical wisdom in evaluation. For the most part, I approach these topics from the viewpoint of individual evaluators, seeing evaluation practice as they might see it.

Values are perhaps the most central concept in professional evaluation. Yet, the conception is fuzzy. If we asked evaluators questions about values, we would find divergent or conflicting opinions (Julnes, 2012, Greene, 2005, House & Howe, 1999). I hope to clarify our understanding of values by addressing basic questions. What are values? Where do they come from? Why do we have them? Why is our conception so confused? How do we handle values in evaluations?

A second key concept is that of biases. People's thinking about biases is not so much confused as under-appreciated. Some of the most prominent evaluation frameworks have focused on biases. That includes the Campbell and Stanley (1963) framework for validating causal inferences drawn from quasi-experimental studies by correcting for potential biases. Another is Scriven's (1972) conception of objectivity in which objectivity is achieved by correcting for biases in general. In addition, research on thought processes has made significant progress by focusing on biases (Kahneman, 2011). Instead of trying to define rules for thinking, investigators examine biases embedded in it.

Evaluating, pages xiii–xiii

A third concept is that of practical wisdom. This concept is less well understood. By practical wisdom, I mean the special knowledge about conducting evaluations that evaluators acquire through their experiences. We misunderstand and under-appreciate the importance of practical wisdom. Practical wisdom informs what we do, possibly as much as theory does. As observers have noted, experienced evaluators often conduct evaluations in similar ways, regardless of their theoretical approaches. That's because practical wisdom in context determines much of what they do. I'll provide examples of practical wisdom and how we employ it.

Throughout the book, I draw on the empirical research on thinking processes. Research on thinking offers ideas for the improvement of evaluation and for possible future research. After all, if both evaluation and cognitive research are basically correct, they should be compatible. Mark, Donaldson, and Campbell (2011) have already taken a step in this direction by drawing on the connections between evaluation and social psychology. Here, I concentrate on connections between evaluation and cognitive research.

Somewhat to my surprise, I've discovered that the research on thinking does provide new insights into evaluation, as well as empirically supporting many evaluation ideas. Although I used some of these ideas in *Evaluating with Validity* (House, 1980), the research has advanced enough that it's more useful now. In fact, it's helped me resolve a few issues that puzzled me for a decade. In addition, following Kahneman's style in *Thinking Fast and Slow* (2011), I've used examples of my experiences in evaluation to illustrate ideas. I found his personal examples particularly persuasive.

The Structure of the Book

Structurally, there are three parts to the book. The first part deals with reframing the main concepts in evaluation, including the origins of our values and biases. The second deals with how we handle values and biases in practice. The third discusses how we learn practical wisdom and use it in evaluations. Each part has three chapters.

The first part of the book, "Where Values Come From," deals with the origins of our values and biases. These three chapters are pitched at three different levels of analysis. The first chapter explores how evaluators acquire values and biases at the personal level and how these influence their evaluations. The second explains how human thought processes work generally, as revealed by empirical research, and how evaluation fits with that research. The third chapter is a Socratic dialogue about learning values as members of communities, how our conception of values became confused, and what the correct conception is.

In Chapter 1, "How Personal Values Influence Evaluation," I examine how we learn values from the experiences of growing up. I use myself as an example by discussing details of my childhood and how these experiences influenced my personal values, my professional values, and my intellectual style. Personal values have had an enduring influence on how I conduct evaluations, the ideas I've advanced in the field, and how I've led my life, including in an avocation of financial investing. These dispositions include looking beneath the surface of things, looking behind what people say, and creating ideas that push beyond consensus boundaries and traditional frameworks. I call such dispositions "having a skeptical personality." Cognitive researchers might call such dispositions, "epistemic values" or having a "reflective mind" (Stanovich, 2011, 2009). These traits serve well in evaluating and investing. They also have downsides.

In Chapter 2, "Evaluating and the Research on Thinking," I discuss the empirical research findings on thought processes, mostly as summarized by Daniel Kahneman in *Thinking Fast and Slow* (Kahneman, 2011). My interpretation of this work, encapsulated in the dual process model of thinking, is that both fast and slow thinking processes are thoroughly evaluative. That is, core human thought is basically evaluative. Human thinking has evolved in such a way that we can evaluate our environment, endowing us with survival advantages.

However, these thinking processes are far from perfect. In order to do fast thinking, the necessary heuristics introduce certain biases. These thinking biases are much the same biases that we worry about in evaluation. In this regard, there is considerable agreement between research on thinking and evaluation theory. For example, "bias," and "framing" are important working concepts in both. And the reflectivity aspect of thinking is close to evaluative thinking, which includes viewing matters from more than one frame simultaneously, plus the ability to change frames (Stanovich, 2011, 2009). I apply these ideas to evaluation practices later.

In Chapter 3, "Reframing Values," I present a model of how we learn values from our community and how the wrong conception of values developed in the evaluation community (Davidson, 2001, 2004). Our conception of values was derived from earlier notions of facts and values. Unfortunately, the ideas that we inherited include the mistaken fact/value dichotomy. The essence of this dichotomy is that facts and values are different entities and that facts can be determined rationally, but values cannot be (Scriven, 2013, Putnam, 2002; House & Howe, 1999). Hence, facts are objective, and values are subjective. The fact/value dichotomy is incorrect, and its lingering influence causes errors. In other words, values have been framed incorrectly. Reframing values is consistent with the research on thinking, contemporary philosophy, and practical wisdom.

In the second part of the book, "Handling Values and Biases in Practice," I discuss how values and biases are handled in actual evaluations. These three chapters describe an evaluation study, discuss the principles that guided the study, and trace the development of those principles. In Chapter 4, "An Evaluation Case Study," I discuss an evaluation in considerable detail, which I use to illustrate several ideas over the following chapters. The study was a monitoring evaluation of a large federal court-mandated bilingual education program in Denver over a six-year period. The social and political contexts of the study strongly influenced what was possible to do. The successes and failures of the evaluation are assessed.

In Chapter 5, "Democratizing Evaluation," I present the principles that guided that evaluation. The approach is called deliberative democratic evaluation, and its three principles are inclusion of stakeholders, extensive discussions with stakeholders, and deliberating on findings with stakeholders (House & Howe. 1999). I also present caveats about using such an approach. In reflecting on this evaluation, I show how the approach addressed thinking biases identified by cognitive researchers. However, my intent is not to persuade evaluators to use this approach, but rather to encourage evaluators to democratize evaluations in general and reflect on their own approaches.

In Chapter 6, "Underlying Values and Influences," I trace the intellectual origins of the evaluation approach back to major influences. These influences include my childhood, family, and schooling; Rawls theory of justice; Barry MacDonald's conception of democratic evaluation; egalitarian ideas from several Scandinavian sources; and the deliberative democratic critiques of the U.S. governing structure. These influences were blended into deliberative democratic evaluation, named after the last influence (House & Howe, 1999). Underlying values of the approach include a strong egalitarianism and the epistemic values associated with "reflectivity" (Stanovich, 2011, 2009).

In the third part of the book, "Practical Wisdom in Evaluation," I address three questions. What is practical wisdom? How do evaluators learn practical wisdom? Under what circumstances is it valid? In Chapter 7, "Evaluating with Practical Wisdom," I analyze the concept. Essentially, it consists of knowing what to do in particular circumstances, of knowing when and how to apply rules and guidelines, of knowing how to improvise and balance conflicting aims, of being able to interpret the perspectives of other people, and of being able to frame and reframe situations to guide actions. I apply these concepts to the Denver bilingual education evaluation.

In Chapter 8, "Learning Practical Wisdom," I explore how we might enhance the learning of practical wisdom. Basically, we learn from long experience in the field. However, this knowledge can be supplemented by learning from vicarious experiences. Case studies, like the Denver study, are one possibility. Another is to learn from fiction written expressly for the purpose of reflecting on the politics and ethics of evaluation. I present an excerpt from my evaluation novel and analyze it to illustrate the substance of what such learning might be (House, 2007). I conclude with examples of how evaluators have used the novel in teaching classes.

In Chapter 9, 'When to Rely on Practical Wisdom," I discuss the validity of practical wisdom and clinical expertise. Empirical research indicates that such knowledge is valid only under certain conditions. One condition is that the environment is sufficiently regular that practitioners are able to learn from it. Many working environments are too unpredictable. The other condition is that practitioners have sufficient opportunity to learn these regularities. Many environments don't meet either of these conditions. In my judgment, the practice of evaluation does meet these conditions. However, practitioner overconfidence about the validity of what they know is a threat. I conclude the chapter with two follow-up excerpts from the novel.

The book ends with a chapter that reviews several ideas discussed in the book. Each idea is a theme that runs throughout. Taken together, these ideas reframe evaluation practice.

PART I

Where Values Come From

Values and value judgments are at the core of evaluation. In 1999, Ken Howe and I published a detailed analysis of values in evaluation (House & Howe, 1999). The book was a discussion of the role of values in various evaluation approaches, including what we thought was the correct nature of values and value judgments. In our view, the fact/value dichotomy caused many errors. The dichotomy casts values as non-cognitive, seeing facts as objective and values as subjective. That's an incorrect conception of values.

Fifteen years later, the arguments in our book are still valid, in my opinion, and confirmed by other work (Putnam, 2002). However, the discussions in our book are mostly philosophic, and not every evaluator is inclined to read philosophy. A few years ago, I decided to present some additional perspectives on values. In the first part of this book, I present three perspectives, a biographical view of values, that is, how values develop in people's lives, a view based on thinking processes as seen by cognitive psychologists, and a view based on the history of how evaluators came to have an incorrect conception of values. These three perspectives offer insights not available from philosophic analysis alone.

The first chapter explores how personal values develop in the lives of evaluators and how these values influence our evaluation work. I use myself as an example, not the finest example perhaps, but one that embarrasses only me. I trace events in my childhood that led to a skeptical view of the decisions adults make. I decided at an early age that I had to judge things on my own. Such an independent, skeptical attitude developed into an intellectual style eventually. In evaluation, I have rethought core ideas, such as validity, values, and social justice.

The second chapter discusses how evaluation fits with the recent research on thinking. While reading Daniel Kahneman's (2011) book, Thinking, Fast and Slow, I realized that the basic cognitive processes he was describing were evaluative thinking processes. This led me to the conclusion that thinking is basically evaluative. Evaluation is not something added on later, but is present in thinking from the beginning. Furthermore, the research strategy employed by Kahneman and his colleagues is similar to that in evaluation. That is, they have studied biases in thinking as a key to understanding cognitive processes. In evaluation, we've focused on identifying, understanding, and preventing biases, whether in the Campbellian validity framework or Scriven's conception of objectivity as findings being unbiased.

Hence, biases play an important role in both evaluation and cognitive psychology. By biases I mean those habits of thought that often lead to erroneous findings and incorrect conclusions. For example, biases in sampling, measuring instruments, interview procedures, and statistical techniques are common in evaluation, and we work to prevent them. I discuss several biases analyzed by the psychologists, such as framing errors, halo effects, and generalizing from incomplete information. I apply these insights to evaluation situations throughout the book. (There is another use of the term "bias" that means something like "preferences." For example, "I am biased toward vacations in Europe." That is not the meaning of biases here. In this book, biases are proclivities to error in thinking.)

Finally, in the third chapter, I use a question and answer dialogue to trace how we in evaluation inherited a mistaken view of values. Sometimes history can inform and clarify. When you're lost, it's often useful to figure out where you made the wrong turn. In this case, we were given wrong directions as to where to go by some of our intellectual predecessors, including philosophers and social scientists. Of course, these scholars had reasons for making such an error, and it's helpful to understand how they came to see values as subjective within their historic context. Hopefully, we are back on the right track. I end the chapter by suggesting possible future directions for thinking about values. I hope the Socratic dialogue helps clarify ideas that have been confused for some time.

1

How Personal Values Affect Evaluations

Over the years I've had the privilege of knowing many of those who shaped the evaluation field. Some have had strong, fascinating personalities. I've seen how their personalities (as I understand them) influenced what ideas they embraced and how they handled evaluations. Not surprisingly, sometimes their ideas about evaluation were different from their behavior. Occasionally, I've wondered what shaped their lives.

Without doubt, professional training and experience account for much of what evaluators do, but so do the personal traits of evaluators. Personal traits and values affect evaluations in ways not easy to generalize. There are many personal differences and nuances in how evaluators conduct studies: how carefully they collect data, how acute they are in detecting discrepancies in the data, how tough they are in drawing conclusions, and how well they get along with others.

Seeing intriguing connections among personal proclivities, practices, and theories, I've been tempted to write about how personal values affect the work of evaluators I know. On reflection, I decided that I don't have that many friends and can't afford to alienate those remaining. I've discovered that no matter how accurate or flattering you think your portrayal of some-

Evaluating, pages 3–16
Copyright © 2015 by Information Age Publishing
All rights of reproduction in any form reserved.

one may be, they usually see themselves differently and think your characterization doesn't do them justice. And, of course, they may well be correct.

Therefore, at risk of self-indulgence, not to mention foolishness, I've decided to use myself as an example by suggesting how my personal values (as I understand them) have affected my own work. This approach has the obvious disadvantages of self-analysis. In other words, it's loaded with possibilities of bias and woefully inadequate self-insight. On the other hand, it has the considerable merit of not damaging friendships. At least the wounds will be self-inflicted. I've explored some of this terrain before in memoirs (House, 2012). This example might stimulate some reflection among evaluators about their own practices and proclivities. After all, as we evaluate others, we should take a look at ourselves as well.

The first difficulty in this analysis is the concept of "personality." Some colleagues commented that I am not talking about personality, but something else. I realize personality is a contested concept, even though I'm using the term in the everyday sense of the word. Others think I am trying to do psychotherapy, psychoanalysis, or some other deep personality analysis. The thought never entered my mind. I have no intention, capability, or desire to do an analysis of personalities in that sense.

I wish to focus on personal values. Values are within the domain and competence of evaluators. Indeed, values are the central concept in the field. Personal values are an important component of personality broadly conceived, but it is personal values I'm interested in and their relationship to evaluating. I want to explore two issues. First, how do personal values affect evaluations? Second, what latitude should be given to personal values in conducting evaluations?

I shall deal with this topic by presenting two talks that I gave for other purposes, both talks dealing with my background and behavior, and then commenting on these talks. The first talk connects childhood events to my career. I then comment on the meaning of that talk. The second talk deals with interactions with a colleague, Marvin Alkin, as we wrestle with investment decisions using our evaluation skills. I discuss how our actions reflect our personal values and the evaluation process. The original talks appear in quotes to distinguish them from the commentary. Comments inserted after the fact are in italics. The final section of the paper is a discussion of acceptable limits for personal variation in professional evaluation.

The Illinois Talk: Childhood Influences

On May 4, 2007, Gordon Hoke and Bob Stake, long-time colleagues going back to my first evaluation, that of the Illinois Gifted Program in the late 1960s, organized a reception in my honor at the Levis Faculty Center at the University of

Illinois, Champaign-Urbana. Many former colleagues from 40 years ago were there. Here's what I said in an informal talk, as reconstructed from my notes.

Up to now I've avoided tributes like this. I told Gordon "no" once by letter and once by phone. After I hung up, my wife said, "You really should do it. It's not about you; it's about other people." Donna is very fond of Gordon. She grew up in a town near Gordon's hometown of Arthur, Illinois, and shares the common small town ethic: Find out everything about everyone else and reveal nothing about yourself. That way, you can talk about them, and they can't talk about you. Then again, what does she care? She's in China.

My resistance to events like this runs deep. Obviously, testimonials are dangerously close to eulogies, and beyond that, there is suspicion. In the first grade, our teacher put a chart on the wall with our names on it. She said, in her best grade school teacher voice, "Children, if you do this, you will get a blue star, if you do that, you get a silver star, and if you do this, you get a gold star!" I thought: she doesn't think we're going to fall for that, does she? To my astonishment, the other kids began falling all over themselves to win these stars. I felt like yelling, you idiots, they're just little paper stars! *Perhaps a portent of evaluations yet to come.*

By that time I was living with my mother, who was doing shift work in a munitions factory, while my grandmother took care of my sister and me. I wore a latchkey around my neck on a piece of string. My father had been killed in a car wreck two years earlier. My mother had no other means of support and no resources. After a few years she married a man from the factory she didn't know very well, and we moved along a lonely rural highway miles out of town. Unfortunately, the guy turned out to be psycho.

At night they would get into violent arguments, and sometimes he would bring out a loaded gun and hold it to my head, hammer cocked. It was a way of threatening her. I don't know if you've had the opportunity to have an experience like this, but it's totally mind focusing. During these episodes my mind was absolutely lucid. I could see that he was deranged, and I sat perfectly still in complete control of my emotions. No crying, pleading, or moving. I didn't know what might set him off. I did think that if I survived, I would never, ever allow myself to get into such a helpless situation again, whatever it took—whatever. From these and other experiences, I developed a strong resolve, a hard edge perhaps, and intense motivation not to be controlled by other people.

Another conclusion I had reached by the age of eight was that adults made bad decisions that could prove disastrous both for them and for my sister and me. My mother was the best person I ever knew; good through and through, actually too good for the world in which she lived. She was in extremely difficult circumstances doing the best she could. My father and his four brothers were the toughest people I knew, but hardly models of prudence, as the police records show. When they were little, they had been sent to a St. Louis orphanage when their own father died of silicosis working in the mines in Southern Illinois. I reasoned that if I could see through adult motivations and anticipate what adults might do, I could protect my sister and myself. She was two years younger. So, at an early age I began looking beneath the surface of people and events, and I looked with suspicion. This attitude evolved into an intellectual style.

Years later, these traits became useful in evaluation. Often, I can see what others do not see, and I will say what others will not say. All people practice willful ignorance to a greater or lesser degree. They choose not to see things—a luxury I felt I could not afford. I pushed willful ignorance back further than most people can tolerate. In books and articles and in high profile evaluations like the critique of the Michigan Accountability System, the critique of the national Follow Through evaluation, monitoring the Promotional Gates evaluation for the Mayor's office in NYC, critiquing the evaluation of Jesse Jackson's Push/Excel program, or as federal court monitor for the Denver bilingual program, I employed these skills.

In such projects I was pressured in various ways, as you always are in high profile evaluations. After all, people's careers, reputations, and livelihoods are at risk. One of the strangest episodes was a review of environmental education in Austria for OECD. The Austrians were so upset with my report that they sent a formal diplomatic protest to OECD. Not every evaluator can say that. (Freud had a lot of material to work with when he analyzed the Viennese.) Of course, I was highly resistant to such pressures. What could they do? Hold a gun to my head? *And behind this, perhaps the thrill of getting into difficult situations and getting myself out again. Another echo of childhood?*

This style also had carry-over into other parts of my life, as in financial investing. In the early 1990s, I decided I might want to retire someday. I believe it was during a meeting in which faculty members talked at considerable length about how important and unappreciated their work was. To my great surprise, when I began managing my retirement funds, I found investing fascinating. In a way it was a pure form of evaluation that culminated in concrete gains and losses, unlike contemplating the inadequacy of Hume's theory of causation. And I was good at it. Investing required skills similar to those I had developed in evaluation. Warren Buffet says 120 IQ points are all that are needed for successful investing. Any points beyond that are wasted. On the other hand, control of emotion is essential. After all, money is a highly emotional issue, though people say it means nothing to them. Watch them lose a large sum and see how they react.

So, in retrospect, I didn't make the same mistakes as the adults of my childhood. No. I made other mistakes instead. Really, you can't see through everything all the time. You can't live without some illusions. You need illusions to motivate and protect you. Decades ago I said that people are able to withstand far less evaluation than they think they can. That includes me.

So I entertained the typical illusions (*or aspirations, if you prefer*):

- Ambition—To change the world and become famous. And we did change education in the Illinois Gifted Program. After 40 years and seeing hundreds of change programs, the Illinois Gifted Program is still the most effective education change program I encountered, a product of the sixties. (*The core idea was teacher self-assessment.*) And our Center for Instructional Research and Curriculum Evaluation changed the world of evaluation. Of course, we learned something else: the world pushes back and changes things back again.
- Romance—To become so intimate with another person the relationship is transcendent and delivers you out of the everyday world.
- Wealth—To have enough money you can do what you want. You can even spend winters in Australia if you want.
- Legacy—As we grow older, we worry about our legacy. I haven't bought into this illusion fully. Partly, because I have been astonished at how quickly the reputations of even the most renowned social scientists fade away. I hope I am wrong about this.
- Wisdom—The one pursuit I can't seem to give up is trying to learn enough to prevent mistakes. Even this little "thank you" talk has turned into a discourse on biography and evaluation. I can't quit; can I?

However, there is one thing I am sure about that is not an illusion. The most meaningful part of life has been the relationships that I've had with family, friends, and colleagues, including many of you here. That's the meaning of life. That's why I lent my name to this last hurrah that Gordon wanted to stage to bring old colleagues together one last time. And while I am at it, I want to share this tribute with Gordon —one of a kind. Thank all of you for coming. Looks like I finally got a gold star.

Commentary: Personal Factors Affecting Evaluation

In the Illinois talk relating my childhood to how I approach evaluations, I illustrated how values and attitudes develop and how they affected my work. From my childhood and family background, I became skeptical about adult judgments and generalized this skepticism to authority in general. When conducting evaluations, I don't necessarily believe what sponsors or program participants tell me, even when they believe what they say. People can be given to illusions, sometimes about themselves and their own actions. After all, we all have to live with ourselves.

I try to validate what people tell me, particularly those at the top. This can be accomplished by triangulating what people at other levels of the organization say and by collecting other data. I have a keen sense of looking beyond appearances towards what may lie beneath the surface. The motivation for this tendency is to develop a deeper understanding of the phenomena with the idea of preventing serious mistakes. Frequently, I can spot problems before program advocates do since they understandably look for the positive. Often, I am able to discover features of the program that are favorable but overlooked. Looking for something deeper is not necessarily negative.

From my family background and experiences, I also tend to identify and empathize with the poor and powerless, rather than with the powerful. Evaluators usually come from the same social classes and educational backgrounds as those in charge, while those receiving program services come from the lower social classes, or else are children, patients, or others helpless to defend themselves. Empathy with the poor and powerless has prompted me to hold strong egalitarian positions about social justice, and I have tried to incorporate social justice into evaluation. Professional evaluators should aspire to be socially just.

Used inappropriately by those in power, evaluations can be instruments of repression and exploitation. I've tried to advance standards that evaluators should live by and have conducted several high profile meta-evaluations that have served as exemplars of what evaluators should and shouldn't do. No doubt, my sensitivity to injustice and unfairness emerged from childhood and family experiences, leading to these ideas and professional activities.

Partly because of these traits, I have been partial to qualitative methods that focus on what people in the program and those receiving benefits have to say about their experiences. Quite often, the perceptions of those close to the action differ substantially from the views of those running and funding the programs, both because those in charge are removed from the action and also because they need to defend the program's value. Often those in charge do not know what is happening, as opposed to what should be happening, and sometimes they do not want to know. Willful ignorance is widespread.

Of course, no perspective encompasses all the truth, and it's the evaluator's job to collect data about programs and outcomes from different perspectives using both qualitative and quantitative methods. When evaluators are too far removed from the program, they don't know what's happening, which means they may misinterpret their data. After all, data are interpreted within the conceptual framework of the evaluator, and this framework may be awry. Often the framework is derived from listening to sponsors or from ideas popular at the time. Arriving at wrong conclusions by misinterpreting data has been a major failing of evaluations. My skepticism applies to both people and methods. No method delivers unequivocal truth. Hence, I am disinclined to accept foundational positions based on methods or ideology. Evaluators need to look at evaluation evidence cautiously and holistically.

On the other hand, though evaluators should consider many different perspectives, values, and interests, and reflect on issues by combining data sources, there is a truth to be arrived at. My position is not relativist, except in the sense that evaluators should consider many angles to obtain the best answer. In most evaluations there is a reasonable conclusion to be reached most of the time, though the findings may be complex and highly qualified. The deliberative democratic approach to evaluation combines several of these considerations, a natural outcome of my long-standing concerns (House & Howe, 1999; House, 2011).

Furthermore, in conducting and critiquing evaluations, I have been bold in challenging the dominant authorities, whether they are in government, social and educational services, or evaluation itself. If I arrive at a considered position not favored by those in power, I expect them to pressure me to change my views, and to retaliate against me personally and professionally if I don't. I am willing to change findings if I have missed something or if the issue is unimportant. However, if the issue is critical, that's another matter, and I can be resolute in holding to what I think is right.

How seldom those in power encounter determined, principled opposition is indicated by how uncomfortable they are with it. People in power expect professionals to play along with them. They realize that a major vulnerability of professionals is their concern about their own career advancement, and since those in power can help and hinder careers, they expect professionals to "cooperate."

This part of my thinking derives from personal and professional experiences and to admiration of my uncles. After my father was killed when I was four, my four uncles represented to me the model for male behavior. They had come through rough times themselves, having been placed in an orphanage and farmed out as child laborers, a common practice in the early twentieth century. Instead of becoming cowed or submissive, they became very tough. Pressuring them or trying to intimidate them was not a good idea. Growing up, I heard many stories about their behavior in such circumstances. When faced with pressures myself, I sometimes wondered what would my uncles do and, more importantly, how they might judge what I did. They represented a standard of courage and integrity I tried to emulate.

In summary, characteristics that influence how I approach evaluations include strong resolve, autonomy, skepticism, questioning authority, looking beneath the surface, resistance to pressure, control of emotion, provocative insights, and empathy with the poor and powerless. Throughout my life, I have seen myself as an outsider, one who observes from the edge and maintains an autonomous perspective. As Arthur Koestler (1964) noted in his brilliant analysis of creativity and humor, new insights often emerge from marginal perspectives. One must apprehend multiple frameworks simultaneously to discern ironies and unexpected connections. I might add that reading widely across many areas provides access to many frameworks.

No doubt, other evaluators share many of these traits. Skepticism, resolve, checking out what people say, and concern about the beneficiaries of programs are not rare qualities. Perhaps it's a matter of degree how robust such traits are; how they are expressed, and how manifested. Evaluators might develop similar traits from quite different backgrounds. Finally, it's important to note that although some of these traits are well suited to conducting evaluations, some are not. Being too critical, too suspicious, too cynical, or too provocative can be counter-productive. I have been guilty of such missteps on many occasions.

THE UCLA TALK: EVALUATING IN OTHER DOMAINS

(Based on "Decision Making via Evaluation: What's Marv's Opinion Worth?" Symposium in Honor of Marvin C. Alkin, Issues in Evaluation and Decision Making in Society, UCLA, Los Angeles, CA, June 3, 2011)

When I first thought about this presentation, I listed several of Marv's qualities that I thought were exemplary. These included sound judgment, generating innovative ideas, developing key concepts, and employing clever teaching methods. Today I am limiting myself to discussing Marv's judgment. Now I know what you're thinking, "Yeah. Yeah. Everyone honored at events like this has sound judgment. Talk is cheap." Indeed, talk is cheap. What's Marv's opinion really worth? Let me see if I can put a number on it.

Each year at the annual American Evaluation Association meeting, Marv and I get together to talk about evaluation and investing. Both of us are active financial investors. In 2007, the AEA conference was in Baltimore. It was cold, and Marv and I had lunch at some cheap restaurant around the corner from the conference hotel. Among other topics, I told him about my investment in Berkshire Hathaway, Warren Buffett's company. At the time the stock was worth about $4400 a share (circa Nov 2, 2007), and I had something like 180 shares. Marv said, "I'd love to own some Berkshire myself, but you have too much money invested in it. You really should reduce your holdings." He reiterated this advice as we left. It's a maxim among investors that they should diversify their holdings and not put too much into any one investment. You never know what might happen.

Now I knew this as well as anyone, but I had become enamored of the company. I had made a lot of money in the stock, and even though I anticipated a downturn in the stock market the following year (a decline that turned out to be the great financial meltdown of 2008, and much worse than I anticipated), I had confidence that this stock could withstand a decline without losing much value. After all, this was Warren Buffett, the greatest investor of our time, running one of the most successful companies of the past 50 years loaded with cash. If the market did decline, I reasoned, Buffett had all this cash to take advantage of it. Berkshire did constitute a large part of my investment portfolio, and I was putting a lot at risk in one basket.

Investment is a lot like evaluation. In fact, I would say it entails a form of evaluation in which you collect information, make judgments, and have results rocketing back around your head, sometimes in short order. Investing is also highly emotional. Indeed, as I've noted before, Buffet says successful investing requires an IQ of only 120. On the other hand, controlling your emotions is critical and sometimes quite difficult. After the conference, I flew back to Colorado thinking about what Marv said. After a few days deliberation, I decided to cut back significantly on my investment in the stock. I kept some of it.

The 2008 financial meltdown was more extreme than anything since 1932—courtesy of America's investment bankers, who evidently are unable to surmount the 120 IQ point threshold. Berkshire stock dropped from a high of $5000 to a low of about $2300. If I had held onto my original investment, I would really have taken a bath. What happens is that in a severe decline even seasoned investors have a strong inclination to panic, and the more they have in an investment the more likely they are to panic as they see their net worth plunge, their future unraveling. Without reducing my position significantly, I would have been having nightmares. Today the stock is the equivalent of $4000 (after a 50 for 1 split). It's still not back to where it was when Marv and I talked.

The interesting thing about this episode is that Marv provided no information that I didn't know. I knew the maxim about diversification of assets. What precipitated my action was his balanced judgment that I should reduce my holdings. Might I have acted similarly for other reasons later on? Maybe, but it's a fact that I did it based on our interaction that day. I calculate Marv's opinion is worth somewhere between $380,000, if I had sold out at the bottom of the plunge, and $72,000 if I had held on to the entire lot until now, give or take a hundred thousand if I had done something in between. This is decision-making based on an evaluation in which the credibility of the information source was the determining factor that impelled me to change my position.

What makes Marv's judgment sound? First, he is knowledgeable and well informed about investing, as he is about evaluation. Second, he considers all the angles carefully. Third, he is not too excitable, at least in this area. He's not an alarmist. And, fourth, he's not overwhelmed with his own self-interest. This last characteristic is critical because a signal danger of investment advice is that the advice is often given to enhance the interests of the adviser not the person receiving the advice. Advisors frequently have conflicts of interest in which they profit from the advice they give at the expense of the investor. I believe Marv's advice was offered with my interest in mind. In my experience, this factor is critical in assessing a source's credibility and is based on a holistic judgment about the source.

Three other features of this decision-making via evaluation process are worth noting. First, the situation was interpersonal. In other words, the evaluation process was conditioned by the interaction of two people. Though I was the one who made the decision, it was a joint evaluative venture. Second, the process was communal. It wasn't simply two people acting on their own. These two people were members of a larger community, the investment community, and were considering maxims of wisdom generated by that community. Marv and I didn't originate the caveats about diversification of assets. We knew this from learning the common wisdom of the community. By the way, diversifying holdings doesn't always work. No maxim ever does. There's always the question of when and where to apply the principle. What Marv and I were considering was whether this was an occasion when this maxim should apply.

Of course, investment decisions can be taken based on other types of evaluative information with certain key features remaining the same. In 2000, I was a fellow at the Center for Advanced Study in the Behavioral Sciences at Stanford, and Alan Krueger, an economist, told me that one of his colleagues, Robert Shiller, had just published a book called *Irrational Exuberance* (Shiller, 2000). This was the height of the dot-com boom in which stocks, particularly tech stocks, had skyrocketed. During 1999, the previous year, I had 20 mutual funds that averaged a return of 50% for the year. In my life, things that good just don't happen. I had become increasingly nervous about the stock market and rushed all over Menlo Park trying to find a copy of the book. I found one and read the entire book immediately on a Sunday afternoon.

What impressed me most was a graph tracking the normalized price-earnings ratios of American stocks over the past hundred years. At the beginning of the dot-com boom, the trend line suddenly took off like a rocket, shooting up at a steep angle. Nothing like this had occurred in a hundred years. Investors call this a parabolic move, a sign of danger in investing since such moves don't last long. The ascending part is the front curve of the parabola, and the other part is the plunge downward. Over the previous hundred years, the normal price earnings ratio was about 16, and the ratio at this time was around 35. Commentators on television were heralding the advent of a new age. But for me, the stark graph was the clincher. In my experience, life "giveth," and life "taketh" away. I was betting on a plunge.

Next day, Monday, I began selling my stocks. Coincidentally, this happened to be the day the stock market broke for the first time in the infamous "dot-com" bust. The graph saved me a lot of grief. I kept ten percent of my stock investments and lost the same percentage on that portion as everyone else, about thirty percent. Fortunately, this was thirty percent of ten percent, not of one hundred percent. Again, this evaluation judgment was interpersonal, brought about through interacting with one person whose opinion I trusted, and another I knew by reputation, both outstanding economists. And, again, knowing the price/earnings ratio alone was not sufficient. I needed to know what the ratio meant in the context of Shiller's analysis of behavioral economics, based on the knowledge of that community. Shiller showed not only that the stock market was greatly inflated but also explained how that could happen.

One final point. The validity of these evaluation judgments is domain specific. Marv's opinion is good within a particular domain. I don't believe I ever asked his opinion about basketball. He might not be as impartial or unexcitable since he is a rabid UCLA basketball fan. Domain specificity is important. To further illustrate this point, staying with investment, one strategy for investing success is to find a small number of people—let's call them financial evaluators—who are able to make outstanding judgments and to be guided by these people. It's a strategy I have pursued. Warren

Buffett is one example. Buffett is widely regarded as the most successful investor of the post-WWII period. He built Berkshire into a great company by his ability to judge the value of other companies. During this period, the U.S. economy dominated the world in manufacturing.

Of course, all that is changing. Manufacturing is shifting overseas to the emerging markets, particularly China, which will be the largest economy soon. In the past several years, Buffett has struggled to find investment opportunities. It's not the same world in which he learned his trade and acquired his investment wisdom. During the 2008 financial meltdown, he did all right. He made some good investments, but nothing like he might have done with the amount of cash he was holding. He later said that during the crisis, "I did not cover myself with glory" (Buffett, 2009). He's still a good investor, but perhaps not as great as he was in earlier times. The world has shifted on him.

Lee Cronbach (1982) once said that a major problem of research findings in the social sciences is that generalizations seem to hold for a while and then are valid no more. Generalizations decay. Unfortunately, as the world changes, it's possible for even the wisdom of great evaluators and investors to decay as well.

Commentary: Evaluation in Decision Making

In the UCLA talk relating my interactions with Marv Alkin and others, my personal traits played out in a different way. Before I acted on his advice, I had carefully judged his advice as trustworthy. This meant that he was knowledgeable about the topic, not overly emotional about the issue at hand, and not too self-interested. Unfortunately, the investment industry is rife with people offering advice in which they have conflicts of interest.

In our discussion, Alkin and I deliberated about whether the maxim of not concentrating too heavily in any one investment should apply in this case. This is an exercise in practical wisdom, that is, how a general principle is applied in specific circumstances. Whether a valid principle is appropriate depends on the situation. As events turned out, we were correct. It's important to see this joint deliberation as an interaction rather than a simple decision. My decision to sell was influenced by my inclination to anticipate something negative happening.

In the second decision to sell stocks to avoid the "dot com" bust, similar traits were apparent. From personal interactions I had determined that Krueger was highly credible and had no conflict of interest in directing me to Shiller's work. (As I write this, Krueger is head of Obama's Council of Economic Advisers. For other views of Krueger, see Suskind, 2011.) Although I didn't know Shiller, his reputation was strong, and his book was excellent. Given my skepticism, before taking action based on Shiller's graph, it was important that he explained how the price/earnings ratio could become so unbalanced. I needed to know the explanation behind the graph. Again, I anticipated the possibility of a negative outcome such as a plunge in the stock market.

Like most people, my values are complex, sometimes seemingly contradictory. For example, I have been both a strong proponent of social justice in evaluation, and, in later years, a successful financial investor. These two activities may appear contradictory. My view is that I would happily give up my personal investments in exchange for a system of social welfare like that in Sweden, a system in which nearly all members of society have wide ranging social benefits provided by the state. Until such a day, I have little choice but to live in the world into which I was born, providing for and protecting my family and friends as best I can. Indeed, any other possibilities are very limited. All professionals in the United States who have retirement plans are invested in market securities, whether they know it or not. (See discussion in Chapter 6.)

Boundaries of Tolerance

In this paper, I've analyzed how personal values, broadly conceived, can affect evaluation, using myself as an example. To some degree, personal values influence the work of all evaluators. How could they not? Given such influences, the question arises whether evaluations can be too idiosyncratic. Are there limits beyond which personal idiosyncrasies threaten the validity of evaluations?

For the most part, evaluators rely on methods, techniques, rules of thumb, practical wisdom, and past experiences. Within such a practice there is room for personal traits, as there is in all professional activities. Medical doctors vary considerably in personal approaches to their practices without diminishing the scientific status of the medical field. The same can be true for evaluation. However, there are boundaries beyond which personal proclivities become unacceptable.

What might some breaches be? One would be when evaluators systematically ignore important relevant data. That would be unacceptable. Another would be when evaluators who cannot abide government endeavors evaluate government programs. Another breach might be with evaluators who are so much in favor of programs for the disadvantaged that they cannot tolerate negative findings about the programs. With such attitudes, they should not be evaluating these programs since they cannot deliver honest evaluations.

I can think of two general types of people who might produce systematically biased studies. One type would be the ideologically impaired. Ideologues by my definition are those who will not accept data and empirical findings that challenge their rigid point of view. The defining element is not that these people have strong beliefs, but that their beliefs are not open to rational argument and empirical evidence. It's not difficult to find such people in the current political environment.

Opportunists constitute another group. They are willing to produce findings favorable to their own careers and fortunes, regardless of whether the findings conform to good evaluation practices. Unfortunately, policy centers are staffed with many ideologues and opportunists, and they produce many misleading studies. Of course, personal values only influence behavior; they don't determine it. People are never entirely consistent in what they do. Behavior is also influenced by context, situation, and what other people do. Personal values are tendencies to act in certain ways, not certainties. People are always capable of surprises.

Thanks to Marv Alkin, Brad Astbury, Gerry Elsworth, Gene Glass, Laurence Ingvarson, Glen Rowley, and David Williams for helpful comments.

2

Evaluating and Research on Thinking

In his book, *Thinking, Fast and Slow*, Daniel Kahneman (2011) describes some ways in which the human mind works, based on the cognitive research of the past several decades. In 2002, Kahneman was awarded the Nobel Prize in economics for research that he and his late colleague Amos Tversky did. Kahneman contends that in the 1970s social scientists accepted two core ideas about human thinking. The first was that people are rational and their thinking is normally sound. The second was that emotions, like fear and affection, explained the occasions when people departed from rationality. Later research challenged both of these assumptions. According to the research, people make systematic errors in their thinking, and these mistakes are attributable to the design of their cognitive machinery, rather than to the corruption of thought by emotion.

The purpose of this chapter is to present the dual process model of thinking that emerged from this research and to suggest what the findings offer professional evaluation, including what we can learn about the heuristics and biases of evaluative thinking. To preview my conclusions, evaluative thinking plays a huge role in the "fast and slow" dual process model of

Evaluating, pages 17–28
Copyright © 2015 by Information Age Publishing
All rights of reproduction in any form reserved.

thinking. Indeed, evaluative thinking constitutes the core of cognitive processes. Human thought is fundamentally evaluative. Furthermore, Kahneman's thinking model is highly consistent with evaluation theory.

Fast and Slow Thinking

Kahneman's primary finding is that there are two processes of thought that complement each other. In the research literature, these two processes are labeled System 1 and System 2 (or sometimes Type 1 and Type 2). System 1 is intuitive and operates more or less automatically with little apparent effort. For example, if you see a photo of an angry woman, you'll recognize intuitively that she's angry. On the other hand, if you multiply 27 times 46, you won't know the answer intuitively, but you will have ways of solving the problem using deliberate methods. This second process is System 2 slow thinking.

System 1 operates intuitively with little effort—fast thinking. It includes detecting that some objects are more distant than others, driving a car on an empty road, and understanding simple sentences in your native language. These abilities are learned through association, experience, and prolonged practice. Some of this thinking is involuntary, like recognizing basic sentences. Knowledge is stored in the associative memory and easily accessed. A special case of System 1 thinking is expert intuition. For example, after long practice, chess masters can look at a chessboard and recognize patterns immediately, fast thinking. Meanwhile, chess novices must struggle laboriously with each chess move; slow thinking.

By contrast, System 2 focuses your attention on solving problems that demand effort and concentration, including complex computations. If you look at the well-known optical illusion comparing the length of two lines, one line with the ends flared out and the other line with the ends flared in, like an arrow, you'll perceive intuitively that the arrow line is shorter than the other. This is System 1 thinking. If you take a ruler and measure the lines carefully, you'll find they are the same length. This second deliberate process is System 2 slow thinking.

System 2 includes behaviors such as bracing for the starting gun in a race, looking for a woman with white hair, telling someone your phone number, filling out a tax form, and checking the validity of complex arguments. "Pay attention" is the motto. These tasks require concentration and are disrupted without it. The number of System 2 thinking tasks that you can perform simultaneously is limited. You can focus on only a few things at a time. Hence, the slow, deliberate effort. To some extent, System 2 can also change the way System 1 operates by overriding intuition.

System 1 operates automatically while we're awake, while System 2 is normally in a comfortable, low-effort mode, with only a portion of its capacity engaged. System 1 offers impressions, intuitions, and intentions to System 2, and if everything is normal, System 2 accepts these impressions as valid. However, when something appears abnormal, System 2 may be mobilized to analyze and deal with the disturbance. It directs attention and searches memory for an explanatory story that makes sense. System 2 also monitors behavior and exerts self-control. If System 1 suggests you say something nasty, System 2 might prevent you from doing so.

This division of labor between fast and slow thinking is efficient because System 1 is very good at what it does. Its assessments of familiar situations are swift, accurate, and normally appropriate because they are based on long experience. System 1 operates with heuristics that enable it to arrive at swift assessments, though sometimes these heuristics result in systematic errors and biases. System 1 has little understanding of logic and statistics.

On the other hand, System 2 is high maintenance. When fully engaged, it operates with continuous and intense vigilance, and this effort carries a high cost. When confronted with difficult mental tasks, the muscles tense, the pupils of the eyes dilate, the heart rate increases, and blood pressure rises. Thinking involves the whole body. Such mental strain is so taxing that it's sustainable for only short periods. Normally, we conserve energy by running System 2 at a comfortable walk rather than a sprint, while System 1 monitors intuitively with little effort.

Kahneman says that this allocation of attention was honed by evolution. Orienting and responding quickly to grave threats enhances survival—System 1. That's its purpose, and it acts quickly in emergencies, even if sometimes responding inappropriately. Though quick, System 1 can detect only simple relationships, such as "These are all alike." It can integrate knowledge about one thing, but it can't deal with multiple topics simultaneously. Only System 2 can follow rules, compare objects on several attributes, and make deliberate choices among options. System 2 can solve complex problems by dividing tasks into easier steps and committing intermediate results to paper to conserve memory. Such tasks include writing a book laboriously, chapter by chapter.

As most authors will tell you, constant vigilance is hardly the way to live your entire life. The cost is too high. Self-control requires attention, effort, and high expenditure of energy. And, although System 2 can override the intuitions of System 1, such intervention brings conflict, which again requires self-control and heavy energy expenditure, a taxing state of affairs.

Jumping to Conclusions

Kahneman explains how the two systems interact to arrive at conclusions, which he pointedly calls "jumping to conclusions." Jumping to conclusions is a specialty of System 1, and System 1 has its own way of determining success. Its basic criterion of success is the coherence of the story it pieces together. The ideas come from the neural networks of the associative memory and from whatever the mind has been primed with. System 1 considers that which is familiar to be trustworthy, and impressions of familiarity are based on repetition. Often, a sense of trustworthiness is derived from sheer routine.

As markers of truth, System 1 relies heavily on cognitive ease and lack of stress. The associated cluster includes good mood, intuition, creativity, and gullibility. The opposing cluster includes sadness, vigilance, suspicion, analysis, and increased effort (Kahneman, 2011, p. 11). In jumping to conclusions, System 1 is insensitive to the quality and quantity of data that give rise to the impressions. Consistency of information is what counts, not the completeness of the information. Hence, coherence gives rise to confidence, and sometimes to over-confidence. The potential for biases and mistakes is apparent. The benefit of this arrangement is that System 1 can arrive at conclusions quickly, even if some may be mistaken.

System 1 readily constructs stories about what's happening because its ability to detect causation is inbred, as is its need for coherence (Kahneman, 2011, p. 13). Contrary to Hume's assertion that we can't see causation, but see only repetition of events, researchers going back to Michotte (1963) have demonstrated that we actually do see causation. Infants six months old have clear impressions of causality, and babies have the ability to read intentions. Of course, sometimes System 1 attributes causation inappropriately; however, most of the time, System 1 jumps to the correct conclusions because it recognizes familiar patterns. System 1 gets into trouble when the situation is unfamiliar, and the pattern recognition is mistaken.

The overall inference process is one of System 1 continuously monitoring inside and outside the mind and generating *basic assessments* of situations. These basic assessments play an important role because they are what the organism acts on. In order to make rapid assessments, System 1 has a repertoire of heuristics that enable quick judgments for action, if necessary. These short-cuts include heavy emphasis on the familiar, judging based on few data points, assessing based on various cues, employing halo effects, categorizing by prototype and exemplars, and attending to averages rather than sums. System 1 often substitutes simpler questions for complex ones, simpler questions that it can answer.

Overall, System 1 is gullible and biased towards belief. System 1 does not see alternative possibilities. Doubt and uncertainty are not in System 1's domain. Doubting requires the ability to hold two incompatible interpretations in mind simultaneously. System 2 does have this ability and is in charge of doubting and disbelief. Its function is to check impressions submitted to it. System 2 catches errors in basic assessments, but sometimes System 2 is too busy or too lazy, and it endorses impressions when it shouldn't. The overall inference process is vulnerable to confirmation biases based on seeking only compatible data, framing too narrowly, and overconfidence. System 2 is in charge of self-criticism, and though System 2 questions and directs attention, sometimes it's too relaxed in checking the basic assessments offered by System 1.

Kahneman characterizes System 1 this way (Kahneman, 2011, p. 105 ff.):

- Generates impressions, feelings, and inclinations that may become beliefs, attitudes, and intentions when endorsed by System 2.
- Operates automatically with little effort and little sense of voluntary control.
- Can be programmed by System 2 to mobilize attention when a particular pattern is detected.
- Executes skilled responses and intuitions after proper training.
- Creates coherent patterns of activated ideas in the associative memory.
- Links cognitive ease to illusions of truth, pleasant feelings, and reduced vigilance.
- Distinguishes the surprising from the normal.
- Infers and invents causes and intentions.
- Neglects ambiguity and suppresses doubt.
- Biased to believe and confirm.
- Exaggerates emotional consistency (halo effects).
- Focuses on existing evidence and ignores that which is absent.
- Generates a limited set of basic assessments.
- Represents sets by norms and prototypes; does not integrate.
- Computes more than intended (mental shotgun).
- Substitutes easier questions for difficult ones (heuristics).
- More sensitive to changes than to states (prospect theory).
- Over weights low probabilities.
- Has diminishing sensitivity to quantity.
- Responds more strongly to losses than to gains (loss aversion).
- Frames decision problems narrowly in isolation from one another.

Compatibility With Evaluation Theory

The Importance of System 1

In Kahneman's interpretation, it's important to understand the relationship between System 1 and System 2 thinking. Most evaluators would likely identify with System 2 thinking. It's deliberate, careful, and sometimes counter-intuitive. This is how most professional evaluators see their craft. However, Kahneman is emphatic that the real hero of our thinking processes is System 1. That's where the action is. He says that if a movie were to be made from his book, System 1 would be the star of the movie.

System 2 is a backup system that catches the errors of System 1 and handles problems that System 1 can't manage. In a sense, System 2 is thinking at a more careful level of analysis, but the engine of thought is System 1. System 1 assembles data and packages them into impressions, causes, and judgments. System 2 checks things over and extends the analysis in some cases.

Evaluating as Core Thinking

My first impression of the dual process model of thinking was to view System 1 as mere information processing while System 2 actually did the evaluating. However, when I looked more closely, I saw that both System 1 and System 2 are evaluative. System 1 is a monitoring evaluation that surveys the environment to see if everything is "okay." It constantly matches information to normal patterns and becomes alerted if something doesn't match properly. System 1 thinking is evaluative.

System 2 is also evaluative. It monitors impressions generated by System 1 and tries to find fixes if something is seriously out of kilter. To some extent, System 2 is meta-evaluative. Both System 1 and System 2 are thoroughly evaluative. In other words, our basic cognitive processes are fundamentally evaluative. The two systems work for a specific purpose, not to process information idly, but to evaluate and react to the environment. In short, evaluative thinking constitutes the core of our thought processes.

Evolutionary Origin

Why do we have such a complex system of thinking? Kahneman traces the origins to evolutionary development. At an elementary level, an antelope on a savanna must make quick basic assessments in order to survive (Kahneman, 2011, p. 16). Quick thinking and action are paramount, even though the system commits errors occasionally. If an antelope spots a lion that's not there, that's a reasonable trade-off for speed if one is there. Fast thinking enhances the survival of the species. System 1's capabilities were essential in earlier evolutionary development, and, indeed, are still essential. Presumably, System 2 came later as an added cognitive layer of oversight to deal with biases and problems that System 1 can't handle.

Evaluating as a Natural Process

If these research findings are correct, then evaluating and evaluative thinking are natural processes. That is, thinking evolved to assess the organism's environment. This development enhanced survival. Thinking thrived because it gave the species certain advantages. Thinking is natural in that it's part of nature and evolution. In this sense, values can be called "natural." Values as a central element in evaluating evolved from natural elements. For me, this resolves a long-standing issue, the ontological status of valuing and values. Are they "real" or simply figments of our imagination that are projected onto the world? According to my analysis based on the cognitive research, values are real in the sense that they are part of the natural world.

Inside/Outside Nature

Cognitive research reinforces the view that we are part of nature, not something apart from it. As discussed in the next chapter, it's not humans *versus* nature, as some Enlightenment thinkers posited, but humans *in* nature. The Enlightenment idea of an external, value-dead natural world that we impose our values on is incorrect. Human values are part of nature, not projected upon it. This means that evaluators are in the real world and subject to the same errors, biases, and pressures as everyone else. The advantage that evaluators have is that they are aware of these biases and how to correct for them.

Causation

Also, according to research, we actually see causation happening. Again, we function as part of the natural world. Hume contended that we project values onto the world and that values don't exist in the world. He also said that causes don't exist either and that we project causes onto the world. In both cases, Hume was incorrect. I elaborate on these ideas and their meaning for evaluation in the next chapter.

Skeptical Mind

Given the fast and slow thinking processes and the fact that we develop knowledge from our immediate surroundings, you can see how someone might develop a "skeptical" mindset. I've presented some of my own biography in the first chapter to illustrate how personal values and understandings might develop, including skeptical attitudes. Such a person might be highly evaluative and heavily reliant on System 2 thinking fueled by skepticism, doubt, and uncertainty. (I plead guilty here.) This skeptical attitude is in contrast to System 1 acceptance, gullibility, and optimism.

Skepticism entails vigilance, sadness, suspicion, and effort. Skepticism has its advantages and disadvantages. Advantages include the ability and tendency to look beneath the surface, to entertain several hypotheses at a time, and to be reflective. Disadvantages include the burden of being on guard constantly, which comes at high energy cost, and taking too long to make decisions for fear that you have overlooked something. (It can take me weeks to buy cheap wine glasses because I have to check all the options.) Being overly evaluative can be counter-productive, especially in benign environments. Skeptical attitudes are most useful in hostile environments, as in financial investing, for example, where conflicts of interest are numerous. Skeptical attitudes are less useful in benign environments.

Professional Evaluation

Professional evaluation might be considered an institutional embodiment of our basic thinking processes. In conducting evaluations, we rely on both System 1 and System 2. We employ System 1 to collect and assemble basic assessments and System 2 to evaluate these assessments, correct them if necessary, and tackle complex problems that System 1 can't handle, using statistics and research designs to arrive at generalizations. One can imagine evaluators using System 1 thinking as they approach a project, forming certain impressions, and deliberately resorting to System 2 thinking to check out their ideas. No doubt, this analysis is too simple, but it demonstrates the connection between evaluation and findings from the research on thinking.

For me, this analysis solves another puzzle. Scriven defined evaluation somewhat formally as comparing an evaluand on a set of criteria to a set of standards. Stake has contended that's not how he or most evaluators arrive at judgments. (Scriven, 1972, 1980; Stake et al., 1997; Stake, 1978). Rather, in Stake's view, evaluators do much of it intuitively. In fact, he has said that he takes positions intuitively and looks for evidence to confirm them. The danger is ignoring negative evidence, of course.

Both Scriven and Stake have seemed correct to me, presenting a puzzle. How can they both be correct? The dual process model of thinking explains this puzzle as emphasizing either the intuitive or the analytic. Stake emphasizes how evaluators pull together impressions intuitively, and Scriven emphasizes the analytic side; for example, what are the proper criteria? Have I measured them properly? Did the program cause these outcomes? Have I ignored certain biases?

Analyzing Biases

The connections between professional evaluation and the research on thinking are extensive. After all, if both fields are basically correct, and if human thinking is evaluative, the two fields must share many insights. And this seems to be the case. For example, researchers like Kahneman and Tversky and evaluators like Campbell and Scriven have approached their respective disciplines by studying thinking biases. Kahneman spends much of his book analyzing systematic biases that emerge in human thought processes. Campbell and Stanley's internal and external validity scheme is one of reaching causal inferences from quasi-experimental studies by identifying potential biases and mitigating their effects (House, 2011). Scriven framed his conception of evaluation by looking for biases that might affect outcomes. Being objective means being without biases, and evaluators can pursue objectivity by correcting for biases in general. If you think about how large a role biases play in evaluation, both in evaluation theory and practice, you can appreciate how central the concept is in the field.

Some biases that both evaluators and researchers recognize include improper framing, such as casting evaluation criteria too narrowly; relying on incomplete evidence, such as omitting critical data from the study; seeking only data that confirm, such as halo effects and failing to look for negative instances; improper priming, such as being directed mostly by information from the sponsor and program director; and over confidence about conclusions.

Framing

Framing is particularly interesting, a key concept shared by research, evaluation, and practical wisdom in general. We have a common understanding of framing, such as "spinning" events in politics. And cognitive research puts framing at the center of our thinking. The basic principle of framing is the passive acceptance of the formulation given. The frame presented is taken as the focus of thought, and all thinking derives from it rather than from alternative frames. The frame that dominates thinking is usually the most easily constructed model that represents only one state of affairs and minimizes effort. In the view of researchers, humans are "cognitive misers" when it comes to thinking. Reframing requires more cognitive effort (Stanovich, 2011, p. 67).

Many frames carry considerable built-in emotion. For example, when retailers offer a lower price to buyers purchasing products with cash rather than using credit cards, credit card companies insist that the difference in price be called a "cash discount" rather than a "credit surcharge." They know that loss aversion in people is so strong that buyers are more likely to forgo a discount than accept a surcharge, though the actual amount is the same. Similarly, even medical professionals are likely to prefer a medical treatment that offers a 90% survival rate rather than one that offers a 10% mortality rate, although the substance is the same. Such is the power of framing.

Kahneman notes, "Your moral feelings are attached to frames, to descriptions of reality rather than to the reality itself. The message about the nature of framing is stark.... Our preferences are about framed problems, and our moral intuitions are about descriptions, not about substance. Not all frames are equal, and some frames are clearly better than alternative ways to describe (or think about) the same thing" (Kahneman, 2011, 370–371).

I discussed framing effects extensively in my *Evaluating With Validity* book (House, 1980), which employed the "truth, beauty, justice" framework for judging the validity of evaluations. Many embedded ways of thinking fall under the "beauty" rubric, including framing. For example, I illustrated how the drinking driver research changed the *image* of the drinking driver from that of a social drinker who had one drink too many to that of a falling down drunk. This change to a powerful image resulted in strong legislation. Obviously, the image of a falling down drunk driver has strong emotional overtones that resulted in action.

Later, I illustrated that the core idea structure of Rossi, Freeman, and Wright's (1979) popular evaluation textbook was based on underlying industrial metaphors of programs as machines, assembly lines, and pipelines (House, 1983). The underlying metaphors have implications for the criteria chosen to evaluate programs and for what the conception of a social program is. The metaphors frame the problem. In this case, they implicitly emphasize the connectedness, articulation, and coordination of programs, or their lack.

I also analyzed in *Evaluating With Validity* how stories and plots are necessary in shaping evaluation reports, an idea that cognitive research strongly corroborates. When people try to understand phenomena, there is a ubiquitous search for causes and coherence framed in stories. In fact, coherence is the primary criterion by which System 1 judges validity. Framing is not simply about the aesthetic appearance of evaluations, but also shapes the content, often implicitly. It's interesting that ideas that originally came from rhetoric and literary theory centuries ago have been discovered and confirmed by empirical research from contemporary cognitive science.

Several articles in Mark, Donaldson, and Campbell's (2011) book of readings connect social psychology directly to evaluation. Kahneman doesn't remark on the connections of his research to professional evaluation or mention the field of evaluation. The connections to evaluation I've drawn are my interpretations, not his. However, I suspect he would agree. In my opinion, there is considerable potential in exploring these interrelationships. In later chapters, I apply these findings to actual evaluation studies.

The Tri-Process Model

Finally, Stanovich (2011, 2009) has contended that System 2 processing should be further divided into algorithmic and reflective thinking for a tri-process model of thinking. In his view, algorithmic processing is what intelligence tests measure. Reflective processing is what some call critical thinking, not measured by standardized tests. Because they play a critical role in evaluation practice, it's worth noting what Stanovich calls reflective thinking dispositions:

> ... the tendency to collect information before making up one's mind, the tendency to seek various points of view before coming to a conclusion, the disposition to think extensively about a problem before responding, the tendency to calibrate the degree of strength of one's opinion to the degrees of evidence available, the tendency to think about future consequences before taking action, the tendency to explicitly weigh pluses and minuses of situations before making a decision, and the tendency to seek nuance and avoid absolutism. (Stanovich, 2011, p. 36)

I have another disposition to add. Ordinarily, evaluators have a single framework that they employ in conducting evaluations. And they employ this template using what researchers call algorithmic thinking, the thinking that intelligence tests measure; in addition, reflective thinking entails being able to perceive, consider, and act on two or more frameworks simultaneously and to reframe situations when advantageous.

Flexibility in framing and reframing is a critical aspect of rationality. Experienced evaluators should be sophisticated enough to use multiple frameworks to guide them though projects instead of relying on one template. Reality is sometimes too complex to be captured by a single framework. In a sense, reflectivity is a supra-evaluative set of skills that supplements and cross checks the evaluator's approach, much as engineers build backup systems into complex designs.

For example, in *Evaluating With Validity*, I expanded the concept of validity by contending that evaluations should be true, coherent, and just

(House, 1980). Untrue, incoherent, and unjust evaluations are invalid. I explained these three dimensions, with truth determined through argumentation, coherence manifested in images, stories, and metaphors, and justice exercised through principles of social justice. Each dimension entailed a different framework. The reframed conception of validity consisted of multiple frames held in mind simultaneously. Although multiple framing sounds overly complex, we employ multiple frameworks all the time when we engage in conversations with others. We have great capacity for doing so, even when it's not highly developed. In the *Validity* book, I showed how imagery, metaphor, story, and coherence are used in evaluations. Some ideas I borrowed from semantics and literary theory. Since then, cognitive research has provided empirical support.

These reflective thinking processes include goal management, epistemic values, and epistemic self-regulation. These dispositions underlie an important aspect of overall rationality. In the previous chapter, I illustrated how skeptical tendencies might develop in individuals at an early age and persist through life. In the second part of this book, I emphasize these dispositions when considering how we conduct evaluations.

3

Reframing Values

Reader: *Wait a minute. Wait a minute. Where are you going with this? First, you talk about how you learned certain values in your childhood that influenced how you conduct evaluations. Then you connect evaluating with our core thought processes. That's pretty big range of topics.*

House: What I'm trying to do is reframe how we think about values in evaluation, including where they come from and how we use them. From one perspective, values come from our personal backgrounds, such as from our childhoods. From another perspective, an evolutionary perspective, values have evolved as a critical part of human thought processes. Our core thought processes are fundamentally evaluative. In this chapter, I want to look at values and the community.

Ok, then, answer this question. What are values?

Values are beliefs about the worth of something, whether something is good or bad. Similarly, facts are beliefs about how the world is. When facts are undisputed, we see them as how things "really are." Ultimately, though, facts are beliefs, and beliefs can be wrong and change over time. No matter how widely held, beliefs might be proved wrong later. Values are also beliefs that may be right or wrong. What we think is worthwhile might not be when we discover more about it.

Where do values come from? You talked about growing up. But that's just you.

We learn values from interacting with the people around us—our family, friends, and community—and from interacting with the world. That's what I did as a child. We grow up sharing the world with other people, and we learn about the world by interacting with them. By comparing our thoughts to other people's words and actions plus what we see, we develop beliefs about the world and about other people. By comparing our thoughts to what other people say and do, we come to think that our thoughts are similar to theirs. In other words, we share a community.

Well, that's just common sense.

Yes, it is. The philosopher Donald Davidson (2001, 2004) developed a simple model to indicate how this might happen. His model is based on how someone interprets a new language without having a dictionary of terms. At the simplest, a foreign speaker points to an object and names it. The learner reasons that the speaker is naming the object and attaches the name to the object. The learner, by comparing his/her thoughts to the speaker's words and actions, comes to understand the language. Generalizing this model to growing up, we learn language along with the facts and values of those around us, and we learn these things holistically. Interacting with others is critical, and learning is communal. We learn the facts and values of our community from our community.

You can generalize this process?

Yes, to an extent. The basic source of knowledge is interpersonal communication. Indeed, communities of minds are the basis for all knowledge and provide the meaning of things. Through interpersonal communication, we generate ideas and check their meaning. In Davidson's model, a person interpreting the world engages in three modes of knowing: knowledge of self, knowledge of the world, and knowledge of others. All three modes of knowledge are essential for a complete picture. No type is more fundamental. Interpreting the world involves a holistic process of mixing and matching perceptions while communicating with those around us.

Come on. It can't be that simple!

No, of course not. No doubt, learning about the world and other people is more complicated. Other theorists, like Vygotsky (1978) and Giddens (1984), tackle these issues in detail. But the interpretive model provides insights by integrating ideas that we know from other sources. Learning is interpersonal. It consists of interacting with others and the world. And it's communal. The community is the basis of knowledge. Furthermore, we learn facts and values all mixed up together holistically.

The interpretive model also suggests how beliefs can become imbued with emotion. Beliefs are closely associated with the people that we learn from as children, including our family, friends, and community. As we match our responses to others and infer causes, we attribute coherence, correspondence, and logical consistency to other speakers and to the beliefs we're constructing. We don't expect speakers to keep changing the names of objects. Otherwise, learning meanings would be incomprehensible.

Is knowledge like this reliable? What we learn from the community?

As learners, we take the knowledge from the community to be correct, for the most part. After all, if it's communal knowledge, it's been around for a while and is more or less consistent with other information. Which is not to say it can't be wrong. Normally, though, you would expect facts and values to be accepted uncritically. You wouldn't expect this knowledge to be contested unless there was a disruption of some kind. You might also expect that some core beliefs that have been around for a while would be cherished as wisdom, about what's worthwhile. Some values might even be celebrated within the community.

Come on. What's this have to do with professional evaluation?

O.K. Values are the core of evaluation. Values are critical to evaluating anything. In our profession, we evaluate programs and other entities in terms of core values or values derived from them. Values appear in all aspects of evaluation. In the criteria we use to evaluate, in the processes, procedures, and methods we use to collect and analyze data, in the personal values of evaluators and stakeholders, and in the values of the evaluation community itself. Evaluators as evaluators bring scholarly values to bear. Scholarly values include coherence, consistency, rationality, and criticality. These values are more central in professional evaluation than in ordinary life.

I thought values were emotional?

Values can be emotional, but not necessarily so. Love of family is likely to be felt emotionally, for most of us. However, value claims like "Follow Through is a good educational program" or "BMWs are good cars" are not highly emotional for most people. Facts can also be emotional, though we don't think of them that way. For example, if you're in a doctor's office and hear an MD tell someone, "You have six months to live," most of us are likely to feel that exchange emotionally, even if the patient's a stranger. Since values are about what's worthwhile, and since we learn them from close associates, values are often imbued with emotion. But not all value claims are emotional, and not all facts are unemotional.

But, aren't values subjective whereas facts are objective?

No, not really. Certainly, we can distinguish between facts and values at some level. For example, "The sun comes up every day" is a factual claim. "It's good that the sun comes up every day" is a value claim. We can discern a difference between these two statements. However, both statements are beliefs. "The sun comes up every day" is objective, but "It's good that the sun comes up every day" can also be objective. Both beliefs can be objective in the sense they can be confirmed by rational analysis. We can assemble credible evidence for the validity of both statements. In the sense that both can be rationally assessed, both statements can be objective.

Of course, there are differences between the two statements. For example, you can *see* the sun rising in a way that you can't see the sun rising being a good thing. And this difference has caused some to assert that value statements are not objective because you can't see them. Seeking a foundation for beliefs in visual images has led to a mistaken view of values as being subjective. Actually, the critical distinction is whether values are cognitive or non-cognitive, whether we can reason rationally about them.

Well, that's not what I learned in grad school.

No, me either. I learned what most of us did at that time—that value judgments are subjective, irrational, and possibly emotional. I used to think that values are subjective and that facts were objective. That was consensus knowledge. The distinction seemed right because that's what I was taught. One of my early papers was based on Israel Scheffler's (1967) work distinguishing between the "context of discovery" in science, which is non-cognitive, and the "context of justification," which is cognitive. That distinction reflects a non-cognitive view of values.

I gradually changed my view by talking to Michael Scriven, reading his work and that of other philosophers (Scriven, 1969, 2013). Most philosophers these days would not hold to the view that values are subjective, meaning that values are non-cognitive (Putnam, 2002). As a philosopher of science, Scriven dealt in these ideas, and also tested these concepts against life activities. For example, being a car buff, he compared everyday evaluative judgments about consumer products to philosophic concepts. Some concepts didn't hold up. The view of values as subjective didn't hold true.

Philosophers often generate interesting ideas that don't fit reality. Zeno's paradox is an example. The paradox is that since you can only get halfway to the door from where you are, then only half of the distance that's remaining, and so on ad infinitum, you can never get out the door because you can only go halfway each time. This paradox provided entertainment and possibly a livelihood for philosophers for centuries.

However, I doubt there are many philosophers sitting around in rooms unable to leave. Unfortunately, the miscasting of the nature of values has not been benign. It's caused serious damage to the social sciences by casting them as value-free.

The mistaken view of values is that they are non-cognitive?

The mistaken conception is that facts and values are different kinds of entities altogether. Facts are objective, and values are subjective and cannot be rationally assessed. Hence, values are non-cognitive. If they were cognitive, they could be tested rationally. In philosophy, this mistaken belief is called the fact/value dichotomy. The fact/value dichotomy is a metaphysical claim that facts and values are two different kinds of things.

Well, what difference does it make?

This is where much of the confusion and disagreement about values arises. The view that value claims can't be subjected to rational analysis can lead to serious errors in conducting evaluations. It can lead to evaluators failing to assess key outcomes of programs, to focusing on the wrong outcomes, and to ignoring powerful forces influencing evaluations, like the biases of evaluators or the politics of the situation. It can lead to false findings.

I don't get it. Why were we taught this view of values if it's wrong?

There are two aspects to how such a mistake occurred. One aspect concerns the original ideas. The other is about the circumstances that sustained the original mistake. Ideas are born out of particular times and contexts, and if they flourish, they must serve the purposes of others. The original ideas were formulated by David Hume (1739/1978). In tracing the history of the fact/value dichotomy, Hilary Putnam put it this way: "The idea that 'value judgments are subjective' is a piece of philosophy that has gradually come to be accepted by many people as if it were common sense....Value judgments according to the most extreme proponents of a sharp 'fact/value' dichotomy are completely outside the sphere of reason" (Putnam, 2002, p. 1). In *The Collapse of the Fact/Value Dichotomy*, Putnam shows why the fact/value dichotomy is incorrect and how it has seriously damaged the social sciences.

Hume's idea was based on his notion of what a "fact" was. He had a pictorial semantics of the world. In this conception, you must have an image in your head that resembles what's out there. If you can't see it, or have a "sensible impression," it's not a fact. It's not real. If you can't see values, they're not facts. Hume did think that the moral "sentiments" were important, but they should be dealt with in other ways. He even wrote about the "moral sentiments." But they weren't facts in his objective world. They were closely connected to emotions.

Yeah, I can see the visual image idea.

Incidentally, Hume used similar arguments against causation. In his view, causation isn't factual because you can't see it either. For example, when you see a billiard ball hit another, you don't see "causation," you just see succeeding events, one ball hitting the other and the other rolling away, according to Hume. Causation and values are projections from your mind. Interestingly, people bought the idea that moral sentiments were not facts, but many didn't buy the causation argument. Maybe it's because that didn't serve their purpose. Of course, Hume was wrong about causation, too. According to cognitive researchers, we do see causation.

But, come on, we don't waste our time reading Hume anymore. How could his ideas affect social science?

The ideas went through many thinkers from Hume to us, and they got transformed along the way. No need to go into the long history. The impact on social science came mostly from the positivists. The logical positivists in the early twentieth century, notably Rudolf Carnap (1934) and the Vienna Circle, influenced the social sciences strongly. Karl Pearson's work (1911) was also highly influential. The social sciences were in their formative years at the time.

Long after Hume, the positivists still held to the dichotomy of facts and values, but it became increasingly difficult to argue that facts were things you could see. By this time, scientists had discovered bacteria, nuclear particles, and even curved space. Above all, the positivists wanted to be scientific and, in fact, envisioned themselves as defining the logic of the scientific method. With some consternation, they eventually concluded that facts were what turned out to be valid in scientific theories, and that many scientific entities are not things you can see.

What about values? What happened to values?

Well, the fact/value dichotomy was based on what facts were thought to be. The positivists dismissed values since they weren't subject to scientific verification. "Verification" was their term. The positivists didn't engage in serious discussions of value claims. It was all about their idea of facts. To be fair, the discussion of values from Hume onward was almost exclusively about ethics and morals—particular types of values. Philosophers assumed those were the values everyone was interested in. Carnap dismissed what he called "regulative ethics" as "nonsense."

After all, ethics and morals do tend to be prescriptive. And "regulative ethics" doesn't sound all that appealing, does it? This descriptive/prescriptive distinction blended into the fact/value dichotomy. Facts were descriptive, and values were prescriptive. After all, we can't tell people what to do, can we? Carnap dismissed ethics and value judgments as "meaningless" because they were "non-verifiable" in the positivist sense. This was somewhat embarrassing because key positivist terms, like "cognitively meaningful" and "nonsense," were not observation terms, or scientific theory terms, or logical/mathematical terms. That meant that positivists should have dismissed their own ideas as meaningless as well.

Didn't anyone challenge them on these ideas?

Yes, eventually. Quine's (1962) critique perhaps was decisive in finishing off positivism. Scriven (1969, 2012, 2013), another critic, also noted several things wrong with positivist theories. Critics pointed out that many value judgments were not morals, ethics, or prescriptive. For example, suppose an automotive expert claims, "BMW is the best car ever made." This value judgment may be true or false, but that doesn't necessarily mean you should buy a BMW. Or, if an historian says, "Napoleon was a great general," this statement is a value judgment, but it's not prescriptive. Most value judgments that we evaluators deal with are not prescriptive. Pointing out flaws in programs doesn't necessarily prescribe what should be done about them. Nonetheless, values got labeled as prescriptive.

But, why did the social scientists buy into the positivist view?

The social sciences were just beginning, and they were struggling for legitimacy. Social scientists desperately wanted to be seen as scientific, and here were philosophers who claimed to be defining the logic of the scientific method. The positivists were selling something social scientists wanted. There was strong motivation to be "real scientists" like the physicists. In fact, many believed that using quantitative methods was what differentiated the physical sciences as sciences. In the minds of many, quantitative methods became associated with being scientific and objective (Toulmin, 2001). In the minds of some, that's still the case.

Another important contributing factor was the political climate. As you may remember, Max Weber admonished sociologists to be "value-free" because the government might cut off their funding (Scriven, 2012). This may be or may not be pragmatic career advice, but it has little to do with whether value claims can be rationally assessed.

Weber. Well, that's Germany. What do you expect?

Unfortunately, fear was more pervasive than that. In the United States, from the days of the Robber Barons to the "Red Scare" following the Russian Revolution, American social scientists were fired for espousing what were seen as leftist sympathies, such as approving of labor unions or opposing child labor. After all, financial moguls served on university boards and were big contributors. Take a look at the histories of social science, especially that of Dorothy Ross (Ross, 1991, House, 1993). The Cold War against Communism reignited the threatening political climate. Many social scientists avoided expressing opinions that could prove politically dangerous.

That's not very flattering to social scientists.

Social scientists and evaluators are subject to the same political forces as everyone else, and they behave much the same way. More positively, there's also the motive of humility. Some truly believed they were being culturally imperious in analyzing value positions. This is particularly relevant if you think values are prescriptive. How could social scientists tell others what to do? Most of us don't believe that we have the authority to tell others what religion or political party they should embrace. Actually, these are not the things that we evaluate. Professional evaluators are engaged in determining the worth of educational and social programs. For all these reasons, "value free" social science was attractive. Of course, there are places in the sciences where prescriptive value judgments and ethics are necessary. You can't have much of a science if it's permissible to falsify data, can you? That's a value judgment.

I'm lost. Where are we?

Ok, let me summarize. Both facts and values are beliefs, but with different emphases. We learn facts and values as we grow up by interacting with the world and those around us. We learn these things holistically. Facts and values come from our backgrounds, families, education, and community. And our facts and values can be wrong. However, mostly they are correct because they are consistent with the bulk of our knowledge. We don't usually question them unless there's a pressing reason. On occasion, we do want to assess them critically. Sometimes we want to ascertain how worthwhile programs and policies are by subjecting them to close examination. Professional evaluators employ methods accepted by the evaluation community to do so, and in doing so, merge facts and values into evaluative conclusions.

However, there's a lingering confusion. We learned an incorrect idea of what facts and values are. The fact/value dichotomy holds that facts and values are different kinds of entities. In short, facts are objective, and values are subjective. Facts can be determined rationally, but values can't be rationally assessed. Facts are what the world is about, but values are connected to emotions and projected onto the world.

This idea can generate errors in evaluations. It suggests that you can't do what you have to do when you evaluate (i.e., make value judgments). The correct conception is that facts and values are beliefs that can be wrong, and both can be assessed rationally by assembling evidence. Rather than a dichotomy, it's more useful to think of facts and values as lying on a continuum with facts at one end and values at the other. In the middle are statements blending the two

(House & Howe, 1999). For example, "Follow Through is a good educational program" is an evaluative claim that can be critically analyzed by examining the underlying facts and values that support the evaluative conclusion.

Hard to believe one person like Hume could cause all this trouble.

It was about more than Hume really. Hume formulated ideas in the spirit of his times. His mind set had its beginning in the Enlightenment conception of a self-defining human set against the natural world, as noted by Charles Taylor (Taylor, 1975; Lovibond, 1983). The radical Enlightenment worldview conceived humans as set against a "value-dead" objective world. Humans projected value onto the world. That's where values came from.

In this view, meaning, expression, and purpose were features of only our minds. They were banned from being part of objective reality by the presumed dualism of humans vs. nature. Actually, we should see humans in the world, as part of the natural world rather than set against it. Thinking and evaluating evolved as an integral part of human evolution, as I presented in the last chapter. That's where we fit, inside nature rather than outside it. That's the proper framing of values.

Why in the world would the Enlightenment thinkers do that?

Because of the deistic worldview they were pushing away from. Sometimes thinking is about what you're trying to get away from as much as where you're going. Prior to the emergence of modern science, the Church and its doctrines dominated the Western world. The "Great Chain of Being" had God at the top of the hierarchy, with humans, animals, and everything else ordered in their proper places. The meaning of life and the world derived from God's grand scheme.

By contrast, in the radical Enlightenment view, natural science was at the center. The world was a mechanistic place, no more "final causes," sacred numbers, and other medieval concepts. There was no place for value in this mechanistic world. However, the Enlightenment thinkers couldn't shake the human centric view. Humans were set aside as a special category versus nature. Humans projected value onto the world, as they had projected "final causes" in the old scheme. This dualistic frame of humans versus nature generated all kinds of problems and puzzles for hundreds of years, including the fact/value dichotomy.

Ah, thanks, but I've got a bad headache. Maybe I know too much about the Enlightenment already.

Do I detect a hint of sarcasm? Maybe we should look at how we conduct evaluations and handle the values and biases in them. Let's go to the second part of the book.

Appendix: Are Values "Real"?

I recommend this appendix only for those who have been particularly in-terested in philosophic discussions of "realism." (For some background on how the concept of "realism" has been applied to evaluation, see Astbury, 2013; House, 1991; Mark, Henry, & Julnes, 2000; Pawson & Tilley, 1997.) This appendix deals with a long-standing question, "Are values real?" This seems like a strange question. Why does it even arise? In the history of the value concept, philosophers, beginning with Hume, asserted that since you can't see values, they don't exist. If they don't exist in the real world, they must be projected from the mind and, hence, be subjective. "Real" was what you could see out there. Hume also said that causation didn't exist. Of course, the analysis rests on Hume's flawed visual conception of facts. Actually, you do see one ball causing the other to move. Causation is not the subjective projection that Hume posited.

The argument that values don't exist in the real world has been used to support the idea that values are subjective, projections of the mind. After all, if values are real, where do they exist? Can you see them? Of what substance are they made (Mackie, 1977)? The intent of this claim is to eliminate val-ues from rational analysis. To counter such arguments, other philosophers have claimed that reasons and beliefs are indeed "real." According to the scientific realists, something is real if it occupies space/time and/or causes things to happen. We can't see magnetic fields, but we believe they're real because we see their effects. They cause things to happen.

Analogously, the scientific realist philosopher Bhaskar (1979) has ar-gued that reasons cause us to act and that they are real because of that. Human actions are distinguished from the physical order in that they are caused by states of mind, and these states of mind are real. In Bhaskar's view, reasons are analogous to causal structures and causal entities in the natural world. Like other real entities, beliefs (including facts and values) are derived from pre-existing mental material and produced by commu-nities of minds. Like other entities, beliefs are relatively permanent, yet subject to change.

Since beliefs are social objects, they are subject to explanation as to what caused them. In other words, beliefs themselves can be objects of in-quiry. For example, we might try to explain false beliefs. What does this Bhaskar analysis imply for evaluation? Evaluation is a monitoring of our monitoring processes. We examine and transform beliefs through mental work, hopefully making them better. In evaluation, we apply a critical scien-tific attitude to beliefs and reasons, which we appraise by their truth, consis-tency, and coherence. Indeed, I've tried to show in this chapter how a false belief, the fact/value dichotomy, influenced social science and evaluation by discussing its origins and flaws.

Mohr (1999) formulated a different notion of causal reasoning based on the idea that reasons cause us to act through physiological processes, what Mohr calls physical causation. This causal reasoning traces causes the way pathologists track a cause of death by examining the chain of events, akin to Scriven's modus operandi approach. This model contrasts and complements our counterfactual model of causation, which requires a comparison or control group to show what happens when a suspected cause is not present. Mohr's conception is too complex to discuss in detail here, but it illustrates how a different conception of reasons, facts, and values could lead to significant changes in evaluation and social sciences, even in its methods.

What difference might different conceptions of causation make for evaluation? As noted, Mohr (1999) presented an intricate argument for a qualitative conception of validity. Our quantitative conception is based on a counterfactual argument that if A caused B, then both must be present, and that A caused B, if and only if A is not present in the absence of B. To demonstrate the absence of A, you need a comparison group. Mohr bases his qualitative conception on Scriven's modus operandi method of elimination by following causal chains. Mechanics, medical doctors, and detectives determine causes by processes of elimination. For example, determining whether someone died of a heart attack involves looking for physical traces and eliminating other possible causes of death. No control group is necessary.

Another well-known scientific realist Rom Harre (2009), actually Bhaskar's mentor, asserts that it is a mistake to claim that reasons "cause" things to happen. "Causal powers," the sine qua non for scientific realists, reside in the total human being, not in parts of the human. Reasons don't cause actions anymore than arms play tennis or feet run, according to Harre. The entire human organism is the locus of causal powers, often referred to in the literature as "agency." Humans are real entities that cause things to happen and occupy space/time as well.

In Harre's view, portraying humans as "buffeted" about by reasons places causal agency in the wrong place. He says analysts have misapplied a model that works for natural processes, such as atoms being composed of sub-particles, to social processes, where the model doesn't fit. Explaining human actions requires a different approach. Although in the natural world many phenomena are caused by underlying causal entities, in the case of humans, the agency is located at the phenomenal level of the human being. Scientists create scientific models by analogy with other processes, but the source of models for explaining human action should be "social conversation." (I've employed such a dialogical, communal model of human knowledge throughout this book.)

In yet another realist view, Putnam (2004) suggests forgoing ontological analysis of ethics and values altogether. Arguing about whether values are real is unproductive, in his view. Even those who disagree about the ontology of values agree that it's possible to make objective evaluative judgments, regardless of ontological concerns. The fundamental split is between those who believe value judgments can be objective—all realists think that—and those who argue that evaluative judgments are subjective, the fact/value dichotomy.

For what it's worth, my view is that Harre is correct in saying that reasons, beliefs, and values don't cause us to act in the way that electrons cause things to happen. It's the human being who does the acting. Part of this confusion resides in our language usage. We say, "She acted this way because she is frugal," speaking as if the value of frugality caused her to act in a certain way. And, indeed, if someone were frugal, we would expect her to be inclined to act this way. But we also understand that she could have acted some other way and that causal agency resides in her whole being, even if she did act in accordance with her frugality this time. Knowing she's frugal helps us describe, understand, and anticipate her actions, even if frugality is not a causal entity the way an electron is. Frugality as a value does not have free standing causal powers.

In my view, beliefs, reasons, and values are all part of natural processes at some level. I've explained that they are naturally evolved according to cognitive research (Chapter 2). In that sense that they are natural, they are "real." These beliefs have material manifestations, though we are unable to explain them with the current state of our sciences. Humans are part of the natural world, and the social world is part of the natural world, even if it is created by the interactions of human beings and even if social "entities" are not structured like material entities.

All in all, these are significant issues for some, but most practicing evaluators don't have to worry about them unless they want to. The key insight is that value judgments and, hence, evaluations can be rationally determined. Also, in the larger framework, evaluating is part of the natural processes of thinking that evolved in humans over a long period of time. This frames evaluation and values properly.

PART II

Handling Values and Biases in Practice

After Ken Howe and I conducted our detailed analysis of values in evaluation in 1999, we suggested a way that evaluators might incorporate the values of stakeholders in evaluations. Stakeholder participation would make the evaluations more accurate, more just, more useful, and more used, since the evaluations would include the views, values, and interests of stakeholders, and not just the views of sponsors and evaluators. The additional information, properly processed by evaluators, would strengthen and deepen the evaluation.

We called this approach "deliberative democratic evaluation," based partly on the work of political scientists and philosophers. We did not specify particular methods that might be used, but rather proposed the three principles of inclusion, dialogue, and deliberation. At the time we did lack examples. We now have some examples, and Chapter 4 is a detailed case study of such an evaluation. I discuss in considerable detail what I did in the study and the reasoning behind my actions. The evaluation was the monitoring of a federal court mandated program for native language speakers in the Denver public schools. The program was highly contested and politicized before the evaluation began, which made engaging various stakeholders challenging.

Evaluating, pages 41–42
Copyright © 2015 by Information Age Publishing
All rights of reproduction in any form reserved.

Chapter 5 spells out our original vision of democratic evaluation. Since that time, I've expanded my view of what democratic evaluation should be. I believe that any approach to evaluation, even randomized studies, can be more or less democratic. Any approach can include the views, values, and interests of a wide range of stakeholders to some extent. Ordinarily, the stakeholders excluded from consideration in evaluations are those lower in the social hierarchy, that is, those without power and money. The empirical evidence that such groups are indeed excluded in policy considerations is strong (Gilens, 2012).

In my opinion, there is not one democratic evaluation approach that fits all societies and situations. Evaluations must be consonant with the values in the society. Democratic evaluation cannot be imposed on a society. The goal is to make evaluations of all types more democratic whatever methods they employ. There is also an emerging issue of whether a society can be too unequal for democracy to work. The evidence of increasing inequality in the United States and other societies suggests that evaluators will have to consider this issue at some point. I leave that task for future work.

4

An Evaluation Case Study

One way of dealing with differing perspectives, divergent values, and conflicting interests is to include them in the evaluation rather than ignore them. Perhaps nowhere are such problems more acute than in evaluating efforts in which there are strong cultural, social class, and ethnic differences. I'll discuss how I handled an evaluation in which these differences were pronounced. Following that, I'll generalize the approach, noting its strengths, weaknesses, and limitations. As experienced evaluators know, there are no panaceas.

In 1999, I received a phone call from a lawyer representing the Congress of Hispanic Educators. Years before, this group had brought a lawsuit against the Denver Public Schools (DPS) for segregating minority students. The case was well known in legal circles as the Keyes case and originally involved busing students to remedy student segregation. By the late 1990s, the lawsuit had evolved into a case about language and cultural differences. By this time the federal court had stopped the busing of students and required the Denver schools to provide native language instruction to students who did not speak English. In the lawsuit, the U.S. Justice Department joined as

Evaluating, pages 43–57
Copyright © 2015 by Information Age Publishing
All rights of reproduction in any form reserved.

a co-plaintiff with the Congress of Hispanic Educators. Lawyers represented all sides, including the school district, the Hispanic educators, and the Justice Department.

After years of contention and litigation, the plaintiffs had reached a settlement with the Denver schools specifying a required educational program for non-English speaking students. This agreement stipulated educational services the district would provide to these students. The federal judge in the case was Richard Matsch, who had presided over the trial of Oklahoma City bomber Timothy McVey. Judge Matsch, in his Stetson hat, was a familiar figure in Denver. The court now needed someone to monitor the program and report to the court and the contending parties as to whether the district was fulfilling its obligations.

After meeting with school administrators and the plaintiff lawyers, I was selected to conduct the monitoring. My main qualification seemed to be evaluation work I had done involving minority issues in large school districts like New York and Chicago. With the approval of all parties, the judge appointed me court monitor. I envisioned the project as an evaluation in which I was to monitor the implementation of the program, not question the legal agreement. The legal agreement had been settled before my involvement and was beyond my authority and competence.

Language and Cultural Politics

Denver had a school population of 70,000 students; 15,000 could not speak English. These were mostly Spanish speakers, immigrants from Mexico and Latin America, along with a few hundred Russian and Vietnamese students. The Latino population had provided the impetus for the court case. Some students and parents were illegal immigrants who had come to Denver during the boom economy of the 1990s as the Colorado population increased thirty percent, though the legal status of the immigrants was not an issue in this case. Many of the workers building houses, cooking in restaurants, washing cars, and doing other manual labor in Denver were Latinos.

The Anglo business establishment dominated city politics, and the dominant population displayed an ambivalent attitude towards these immigrants. U.S. Congressman Tom Tancredo (representing southeastern Colorado) was a national leader of anti-immigration forces. Furthermore, providing Spanish language instruction was controversial. Earlier attempts had been made to declare English the state's official language and curtail Spanish language instruction. These efforts had failed. The Denver program was called the English Language Acquisition (ELA) program, nomenclature signaling that the program was intended to teach students English, not maintain their Spanish.

The old Latino part of Denver west of the central business district had become so crowded that Latinos were moving to other parts of the city. With the flood of new immigrants, African-Americans, long established residents, were being pushed out of their neighborhoods. Tensions between Blacks and Latinos were high since many Blacks saw the Latinos as taking the affordable housing and under-cutting them for jobs. Political power in the city was shifting as tens of thousands of Latinos moved in. A Latino mayor, Frederico Pena, was elected in the 1980s, followed by a Black mayor, Wellington Webb, and an Anglo mayor after him, John Hickenlooper. When the project began in 1999, Anglos dominated the governing school board, although two Latino board members had just been elected.

To complicate matters, many teachers and administrators in the Denver schools were Latinos who had come from southern Colorado and northern New Mexico, descendants of the old Santa Fe culture. (Santa Fe, founded in 1610, is the oldest capital city in the United States.) These people have a unique cultural identity that predated Anglo settlement by centuries, and they consider themselves Spanish American, not Mexican. Other teachers and administrators were Chicanos, U.S. born descendants of Mexicans who had come generations before.

Many Latinos spoke both English and Spanish and staffed professional positions in the schools and community. Although they identified strongly with the new immigrants and were protective of them, the native Latinos also saw themselves as different. The immigrants came mostly from poor rural villages in Mexico and were uneducated in any language. Among the Latinos themselves, there were ethnic, cultural, and class distinctions, and these differences generated misunderstandings.

As the court mandated program began, passions were inflamed. Over the years the court mandate had been in effect, school district officials and the plaintiffs had deepened their distrust of each other. Each side considered the other suspect in motivation. Some district personnel suspected the plaintiffs wanted to build a Latino political base in Denver; some plaintiffs thought the district did not really want to provide educational services to these students, but only appear to do so.

In my early encounters, these hostile attitudes came through forcefully. Some on both sides told me that the other side was untrustworthy and that I must be careful of them. Furthermore, this distrust was institutionalized in the adversarial positions of the lawyers. Personalities rubbed each other the wrong way: Such-and-such was "unprofessional," "a snake in the grass."

Strong language was expressed privately. This was the political backdrop at the beginning of the monitoring.

The Evaluation Plan

I decided to try to reduce the distrust among these parties by involving the main stakeholders in the evaluation and by making my own actions as transparent as possible. I didn't want any group to see me as siding with the others or as being duplicitous, saying different things to different parties. The circumstances were ripe for misunderstanding. When I announced that I was going to make the monitoring as transparent as possible, one school administrator told me that was a mistake. Why didn't I just act with the authority of the court? The other side had no choice but to accept my findings. In any case, the Latinos were not going to change.

I brought the representatives of the contending parties face-to-face twice a year to discuss the findings of my evaluation and allow them input into the process. Since many participants were lawyers, adversarial by occupation, the meetings had some contentious encounters where one side expressed distrust of the other. Although I set the agenda and chaired the meetings, I could not anticipate what would occur when the parties met. I structured the interaction around information about issues that all of us thought significant.

The 50-page court agreement stipulated how students would be identified as eligible for the program, how they would obtain educational services, how they would transfer to mainstream classes, what resources the district would provide, what the teacher qualifications would be, and many other details. It did not specify how teachers were to teach, only that they must be properly trained to teach English language learners.

At the beginning I intended using data from the district's new management information system to find schools that appeared deficient and visit those schools. However, the installation of the data system fell far behind schedule, and the data system never worked the way the vendor had promised. I had to do something else. One possibility was to survey participating schools by questionnaire. However, my early experiences in evaluation made me leery of such an approach.

Instead, I constructed a checklist based on key elements of the program as specified in the Denver court agreement. By visiting schools, I could judge each school as being in compliance, not in compliance, or marginal on several features of the program. I submitted the checklist to all parties to ensure these features were the most significant ones. People made helpful suggestions, and I visited a few schools to see what collecting data would be like. With more than one hundred participating schools, there was no way I could collect the information myself. Sampling schools did not seem viable either since whether each school was in compliance with the court mandated program was an issue.

I hired two retired school principals from Denver to visit and rate the schools using the checklist. It would have been easier to use graduate students for this task since students would be trained in data collection. But I knew that graduate students would have little credibility with school administrators and teachers. Also, it would be easy for principals to fool the students since school operations are complex and mostly hidden from view. Graduate students would have little warning when they were misled since they would not have an in-depth understanding of the schools or the program.

The two former principals knew how the schools worked. When they were misled by practitioners, they could sense it; they had been in similar positions themselves, knew the program, the personnel, and the students. They could tell when a response didn't ring true. And they would know how to check their hunches. Since they were former principals, the central office trusted them not to be biased against the district. Since the principals were Latinas, spoke fluent Spanish, and had supported the ELA program from the beginning, the plaintiffs trusted them as well. I submitted their names to all parties to make sure they were acceptable.

The principals did lack research experience, and sometimes they wanted to offer advice to the schools, reverting to their former roles as principals. To counter this tendency, I held regular meetings with them to discuss their findings in detail school by school and remind them they were evaluators, not consultants. There were lapses, but it's surprising how well people can assume a role once the expectations are clear.

Working with the two former principals and discussing what was going on in individual schools helped me construct views of how the program was functioning. We had insights into what the program was doing and why it was working that way. For example, we might find that a principal at a school was deliberately undercounting the number of eligible ELA students. Why would the principal do that? My colleagues might suggest that the principal was concerned about losing veteran teachers who had been with her a long time. The court agreement stipulated that when the numbers of eligible students reached a certain level, Spanish language teachers must be introduced to provide instruction in Spanish, which could mean that regular teachers would have to transfer to other schools. The principal was protecting her veteran teachers and her school community. Although we couldn't solve that problem, we could identify the issue and seek solutions with the school district.

Enlisting these two former principals as data collectors was one of the best things I did in the evaluation, although it was not part of my original plan. Not only could they communicate with immigrant parents, teachers, and administrators, they were able to detect when things were awry when I had no idea anything might be amiss. I could never have obtained this knowledge on my own or by traditional data collection methods.

As a further check on our site visits, I encouraged the ELA program staff to challenge our findings when they disagreed. ELA staff members were forthcoming when they thought we were wrong, and we hashed out disagreements face-to-face. When we had serious disagreements, we could go back to the school to clarify the problem. Eventually, ELA staff developed their own checklist, similar to ours, so they could anticipate which schools had problems before we arrived. Later, they established their own monitoring procedures as we stepped back as court monitors. As the management information system improved, I developed quantitative indicators of implementation based on district data. I discussed these indicators with the parties until everyone accepted them as measures of progress. Two key indicators were the percentages of identified students who received program services and the percentages of the poorest performing students enrolled in Spanish language classes (as the agreement required). The development of the information system was slow and tortuous, reflecting how difficult it is to obtain accurate information in school organizations. Data had to be collected at the school level, entered into the data system, and aggregated—easier said than done. Errors plagued the process every step of the way. Problems included untrained personnel, confusion over definitions, and lack of attention. It cost the school district a huge effort to obtain reliable data, but, to their credit, they persevered and eventually managed it.

When the data were reasonably accurate, our indicators showed gradual program improvement year by year. This was important because improvement was slower than anyone anticipated, but yet there was progress. The indicators also showed which particular schools were in trouble. By combining our on-site checklists with the school-by-school indicators, we had a cross check on where things stood, both for the district and for individual schools. When particular schools looked bad, we revisited them, and the district sent staff members to these schools to tackle problems. Problems bunched in certain schools. In a few cases principals were replaced. When schools looked good on both the checklists and indicators, we quit visiting them, unless they had a change of principal.

Complications

Constant change in the school district was a complicating disturbance. School principals were retiring, resigning, and being replaced or promoted constantly. New principals meant a new situation, and we revisited each school that had a new principal. Students constantly shifted schools as well. They dropped out, moved midterm, went back to Mexico, or simply disappeared from the attendance rolls. Some schools had more than 100% student mobility, not unusual in urban districts. Keeping track of individual students was difficult, and the information system had trouble managing, as do those in other large city districts.

More surprising was the rapid change in the district superintendents. In the first six years of the court monitoring, there were five different superintendents in charge of the Denver schools. The first superintendent, in charge when the monitoring began, had been in conflict with the Latino community for years. Within a few months of the start of our monitoring, he suddenly resigned, with no explanation. I never discovered what had happened. A second superintendent with no experience with Latino communities was hired from another part of the country. He lasted less than a year. His style did not suit the school board or the community.

An interim superintendent from within the district took over until a new one could be found. Her term lasted a year. We continued our monitoring through these changes. The fourth superintendent, previously head of the state community college system, became superintendent for three years. He had a business-like approach and was not hesitant in telling principals and staff he would replace them if they did not perform. His attitude prompted recalcitrant principals to push forward with program implementation, especially after a few were replaced. News of a principal being replaced traveled rapidly within the district. Principals were accustomed to running their buildings without interference from the central office. Many Denver school personnel had known each other for decades and were strongly inclined to do things the way things had been done in the past. Superintendents from outside disrupted established and accepted patterns of behavior.

In the sixth year of monitoring, the Denver mayor's chief of staff became superintendent. His background was law, business, and public management, not education. He hired a chief academic officer from New York City, who had considerable experience with English language learners. The new theme was to make the district more academically rigorous. Each of the six superintendents had different styles and goals. Each reorganized the district administration. For example, the superintendent from the community colleges established a "quadrant" system in which four super-districts replaced several sub-districts. The next superintendent reorganized the central staff into multi-disciplinary teams, with each team responsible for working with a dozen schools.

With the arrival of each new superintendent, I had to establish a new professional relationship, give the superintendents time to work out their assessments of my role, help them understand the court monitoring, and figure out how their new plans would affect the monitoring. For example, with a team approach to administration, how would working on these teams affect the operation of the ELA staff? The repercussions of these administrative and personnel changes—new superintendents brought in new people—were not clear when announced.

For the first five years of the monitoring, the main point of stability within the district was an assistant superintendent for special services who had been involved in negotiating the court agreement and to whom the ELA program directors reported. For all practical purposes, he was in charge of the program. When I wanted to discover what was happening in the district, I turned to him for answers. Most of the time he responded; occasionally, he did not. In general, I established a good working relationship with him once he determined that I was trying my best to monitor the program and see that it was implemented, not trying to embarrass the district. When the last superintendent took office, this assistant superintendent retired, and I lost an important inside contact.

After this last transition, the ELA program director reported to the chief academic officer. Of course, the ELA program directors also changed over time. There were four during this period. I admired these people and the difficult challenges they faced. They were responsible for implementing the agreement, yet had no line authority over principals or teachers. They were advisory. They could persuade or refer problems up the chain of command, but they could not order principals or teachers to do anything. Yet, when things went wrong, they were held accountable and sometimes scapegoated. Some lasted a long time; some did not. Establishing a working relationship with each of them was critical for our monitoring.

Meanwhile, I met with interested groups in the community, including the most militant advocates, both those opposed to the program and those wanting Spanish in all schools. I listened, responded to their concerns, and included some of their ideas in my investigations when I could. I followed up on information these groups provided about individual schools. I turned down no one wanting to offer views, though I did not accept their information at face value. I considered holding open public hearings to allow others to offer opinions but decided against it. I was afraid such hearings would degenerate into shouting matches.

As we met with the major stakeholders, mainly the representatives of he school district and the plaintiffs, we addressed the issues they had in mind, sometimes redirecting the data collection. Discussing findings enabled us to help them interpret what was happening, and their opinions enriched our views as to how the program was progressing. These face-to-face meetings became a focal point of the evaluation.

My periodic, written reports, usually three a year, went to Judge Matsch. As court documents, the reports were public information that the local media seized on. At the beginning, I asked the district and plaintiffs how they thought I should handle the media. Bilingual education was a hot topic, and reporters were looking for comments. All parties said they preferred that I not talk to the media. Their experiences suggested the media would inflame the situation and make implementation more difficult. As the court monitor whose boss was the judge, I could do what I wanted as far as making public comments. But I decided to take their advice, and during the evaluation I referred media inquiries to the contending parties and made no comments beyond my written reports. The media accepted this stance, reluctantly. They regularly quoted my reports in the newspapers.

Monitoring Issues

Many issues arose during the evaluation. For example, lawyers representing the Latino educators who had brought the original lawsuit were concerned that students should be taught in their native language until they learned English and that students not be forced into mainstream classes prematurely. They suspected the district was forcing schools to move students quickly into mainstream English language classes. When these concerns were voiced, we paid close attention to the English proficiency level of the students when they were transferred to mainstream classes and to the specified testing procedures for identifying and exiting the students.

We did not find deliberate forcing of students to leave the program before they were ready, according to the written criteria. However, we did understand why plaintiffs felt the way they did. Once students were assigned to special classes, it became difficult to dislodge them from those classes. Moving students into mainstream classes required schools to devote extra effort and attention to doing so. The students formed friendships in their peer group and did not want to transfer out of special classes if it meant leaving their friends behind, even when they had the requisite English ability. When district officials realized the reluctance of schools to move students, they instituted procedures to encourage schools to review students regularly and move them. Otherwise, they faced establishing a two-track school system. We did not find that students had been forced into the mainstream prematurely. Nonetheless, it was an issue for the plaintiffs to worry about and for us to investigate. We never convinced some of the plaintiffs that inappropriate mainstreaming was not occurring.

The co-plaintiff in the case was the Office of Equal Education Opportunity in the U.S. Justice Department. These lawyers were concerned that students receive an "equal" education while they were in Spanish language classes and feared that students might have inferior materials and teaching in these classes. We rated the difficulty of the Spanish versus English materials to ensure the materials were similar and examined the library materials in Spanish. The plaintiff lawyers focused on somewhat different issues.

As noted, the Latino community was divided into distinct groups. Many teachers and administrators were descendants of the old Santa Fe culture and some Chicanos. By contrast, many students and their parents were recent immigrants from rural Mexico who had little formal education. The culture and class differences between these groups affected program dynamics. For example, immigrants often took their children out of school for weeks to return to home villages in Mexico for fiestas, a practice that infuriated the professionals, who saw the loss of school time as a serious setback for the students.

Some parents wanted their children to go directly into English classes so they could learn enough English to get jobs and help the family immediately. Most wanted their children in Spanish language classes first, then English when they were ready. According to the court agreement, parents had a choice as to what their children should do. However, we discovered that many schools did not make these choices clear to parents, with whom they might have difficulty communicating. We attended to whether program options were presented to parents in ways they could understand.

The most militant Latino group in the city wanted full cultural maintenance of Spanish, as well as English. I met with the leader of this group in the café that served as political headquarters in the Latino part of town. I listened to her concerns. There was little I could do about cultural maintenance since the court agreement precluded it. However, I did investigate practices that reinforced her view the school district was insincere. Improper practices in one school often were interpreted as being the policies of the school district.

Sometimes the issues came from us evaluators, the principals and me. After seeing how school personnel were testing the students for English proficiency, I suspected their testing procedures were not reliable. Many people with minimal training were administrating the critical oral test that determined entry and exit from the program. We thought the results would vary widely from school to school. Although the schools could hardly be asked to ensure the reliability one might expect in research projects, neither did the district want widely different standards across schools. The district conducted its own reliability study to see how good the testing was. They were appalled to find how inconsistent the test results were. They instituted better testing protocols administered by fewer and better-trained testers.

Evaluation issues were numerous—how many Spanish language courses should be offered? What should be done with students who deliberately failed the English language test so they could remain in classes with their friends? What was *not* an issue for any stakeholder was how the program compared to other ways of teaching English, like immersion, which some experts think is the best way of teaching a new language. Those who wanted all students in English right away were interested in immersion, but they had already made up their minds. I met with the leader of this group and suggested she read my reports on the program's progress to see how long it took students to exit the program, which was an issue for her. Later, she led an unsuccessful statewide campaign to eliminate bilingual instruction altogether. In summary, the evaluation focused on issues arising from the views and interests of those most concerned about the program.

After six years of monitoring, the program was almost fully implemented, in my view. The conflict seemed defused for the Denver schools for the time being. The opposing parties could meet in a room without casting insults at each other. I'm not saying the groups loved each other, but they could manage their business together rationally. The strife and distrust was much less than when we started. At the same time the plaintiffs were reluctant to let the district out of the court ruling. And they often did not agree with what we did as evaluators.

At the end of the monitoring, the school district had established its own monitoring system. The politics of the district shifted, with more Latino members elected to the school board. In fact, the daughter of the man who had sponsored the original lawsuit became chair of the school board, and the new school superintendent (a lawyer who had been the Denver Mayor's chief of staff and who later became U.S. senator) adopted a strong pro Latino attitude. Under these circumstances, a lawyer for the plaintiffs and the district lawyer thought our monitoring no longer necessary. The plaintiff lawyer had long disagreed with us about whether the district was pushing students into the mainstream inappropriately. We could find no evidence for that, but he thought we didn't look in the right places. With these shifts, it seemed advisable to end the monitoring since one side had gained the upper hand politically, and we had been monitoring for three years beyond what was intended.

I had a mixed reaction to these developments. On the one hand, I wanted to resolve the court case, which was still pending officially, though the presiding judge had retired. However, the district now had no motivation to take the case back to court. Nor did the plaintiffs; they held an advantaged position. Fortunately, even though the court case had not been resolved legally, the district and plaintiffs had reached a new level of understanding and cooperation. There was less need to involve lawyers and monitors. Hopefully, the district and plaintiffs would work things out together without third party intervention. Such evaluation makes most sense where different interests and points of view are pronounced. Time to quit.

Special Features

Before discussing the general approach to evaluation, it is worth noting some special features of this study.

The Evaluator as Agent of the Court

The most unusual feature was that the evaluation was conducted under authority of the federal court. Because of that neither the school district nor the plaintiffs could cancel the evaluation, though they could appeal to the judge if they thought I was performing my duties incorrectly. As court monitor, I could subpoena information, though I never used nor threatened to use this power. I tried to do the evaluation cooperatively, not impose court authority. Nonetheless, the court authority was in the background. On occasion, district officials themselves used the court threat to secure compliance inside the district.

Early on, plaintiff attorneys wanted us to cease making holistic judgments about individual schools. When we visited a school and noted compliance features on a checklist, we (the evaluators doing the visit) estimated whether the school was in compliance overall. The plaintiffs wanted us to complete the checklist without a summary judgment, and let them decide for themselves whether the school was in compliance. I thought this procedure would take too much authority away from the evaluators and that those visiting the school were in better position to judge compliance than those distant from the site. I also knew that under certain circumstances holistic judgments are better than piecemeal judgments. (See discussion in the next chapter.)

If we had let the school district and plaintiffs decide separately whether a school was in compliance, we were setting up conflict down the line; the two parties were bound to disagree in many cases. Better to establish right away whether the school was in compliance from our impartial point of view. This judgment could be challenged if others thought it in error. The school would know its status and could do something about it, the district would know and could take action, and the plaintiffs would know and could disagree. I held firm on this issue and suggested that we go back to the judge and have him decide whether we evaluators should be making these judgments. At that point the plaintiffs backed off, though they disagreed with some of our conclusions.

The Evaluation Was Limited to Monitoring

One limitation of the evaluation was that this was a monitoring exercise, not a summative evaluation. In a normal evaluation, I would have investigated broad aspects of the program. What were the effects on students? How did they fare compared to those who opted out of the program? What were the emotional effects? How did school staff view the program? What did they think would work better? What did parents think was happening? In other words, I would have conducted a broad program evaluation. In this case, it was clear that we were monitoring program implementation only. The court agreement was complete, and the only way it could be changed was to have all parties agree to changes and go back to the judge. No one wanted to open the case again, and serious changes were never suggested.

Another issue was how standardized achievement test scores should be treated. The agreement called for the district to collect test scores and analyze them, though how the analyses and comparisons would be done was not specified. Nor were any standards specified as to what levels of performance students should achieve as a group. Individual students were placed and exited on the basis of specified scores on an oral exam. However, no testing standards were set for the program as a whole. The school district collected standardized test scores and analyzed them by group. In my reports I added my interpretations to what the findings meant, since not all parties were versed in test score interpretation. Not surprisingly, district interpretations of findings tended to be more positive than mine, but still reasonable.

The Framework Was Adversarial

Since this was a court case with plaintiffs and defendants, the evaluation was cast within an adversarial framework. Almost everything we did referenced the contending parties: "The plaintiffs want this...." "The district believes that...." Although there was a written agreement between the parties, the monitoring was shaped by adversarial considerations. In a typical evaluation, we are inclined to think of everyone being on the same side (wrongly perhaps); that was not the case here. The back and forth nature of the adversarial process shaped the evaluation in important ways.

The Court Document Defined the Issues

We encouraged the contending parties, and others, to help us define the issues we should investigate. We had the court document, which defined a universe of potential issues. But with the many issues that might arise, some were significant and some not. This is where the parties had influence over what we examined. We engaged issues raised by local parties, which increased the relevance of findings. We did not try to address national or research issues.

Some evaluators believe evaluations should address issues that contribute to an overall body of knowledge. But the theory on which such issues can be addressed is weak. Findings in the natural sciences cumulate because there are strong theories of substance in these areas. By contrast, social science and educational theories are weak because the outcomes are highly contingent on surrounding influences and disconfirming instances are difficult to specify, let alone discover. Generalizing findings is limited. (See my take on this general problems elsewhere, House, 2001, 1991). In the absence of strong theory, many evaluations typically address issues that government authorities want addressed. This evaluation would have been much less relevant and useful to the participants if we had tried to address national or research issues.

Face to Face Meetings

Face-to-face meetings were key to establishing trust among the parties. At the beginning I didn't plan on twice a year face-to-face meetings since the plaintiff lawyers had to travel from San Francisco and Washington. However, when I saw how the first meeting went, and how vital it was to establish credibility, I made the meetings a regular event. I scheduled meetings for times just after I wrote court reports, so we would have something to discuss. These meetings were critical.

Public Role Limited

In part because stakeholders played a central role in the evaluation, broader public participation was limited. This was something I regretted, but also couldn't figure out how to manage. Both the school district and plaintiffs suggested that I not talk with the media. Media reports about the program were not always well informed in their view. I filed my reports with the court, alerted the media, and let the district administrators and plaintiffs answer questions. This was not entirely satisfactory from my point of view because I could not discuss the nuances of the findings, but I never figured out anything better. If I had to do it over again, I might change this aspect of the evaluation.

Treating People Decently

This may seem strange to say, but we treated people with respect during the evaluation, whether they were parents, students, teachers, etc. Jennifer Greene has written that how evaluators treat people during projects should be an important concern. I agree, and as obvious as such an ethic might be, it's not always honored. It's too easy to assume the role of the all-knowing expert.

Methods

Data collection and analysis were not different from most evaluations. Our data collection would not have met the reliability standards of a referred journal article, but that was never the intent. The data were collected for the purpose of establishing confidence that the program was properly implemented. The contending parties had the opportunity to challenge findings if they wanted. I tried to establish a point counterpoint, check and balance system rather than spend large sums of money on sophisticated procedures. On the other hand, I didn't want the data to be inaccurate.

Long Term

Another unusual feature was that the monitoring was drawn out over years. Originally, it was supposed to continue for three years, but the program implementation progressed slowly. The long time period enabled us to change our procedures, refine them, try out different things, respond to inquiries from various groups, and discuss and deliberate with the major stakeholders. We tried to be transparent, encourage the involvement of key stakeholders, engage issues jointly defined by them, and deliberate on the findings. I think it worked for the most part, though disagreements continued to the end.

Political scientist Janice Gross Stein wrote, "The conflict among these values is often intractable and incommensurable. It is because these conflicts are intractable that we turn to conversation in public space, and to those we choose to govern, to set legitimate rules for a conversation that is not about interests, but about principles and values. The legitimacy of this conversation rests on recognized, fair, inclusive, and open procedures for deliberation and persuasion, where those who join in reflective discussion are neither intimidated nor manipulated" (Stein, 2001, p. 225). That's what we tried to do.

5

Democratizing Evaluation

The evaluation approach employed in Denver is called deliberative democratic evaluation. In this chapter, I'll describe what deliberative democratic evaluation is and suggest some caveats in implementing it. After that, I'll examine how this approach mitigates some of the biases studied by cognitive researchers. My purpose is to democratize the practice of evaluation in general. The deliberative democratic evaluation approach is only one way of doing so. The main idea is that by including the views, values, and interests of those invested in the study, evaluation can be more fair, accurate, and just. Also, evaluation findings are more likely to be understood and used. To some extent, evaluators can democratize any study, regardless of the basic methods used.

Deliberative democratic evaluation has three principles: inclusion of stakeholder views, values, and interests; dialogue with and among evaluators and stakeholders so they better understand one another; and extended deliberation with and by all parties (House & Howe, 1999, 2000; Howe & Ashcroft, 2005; House, 2012.). The approach encourages the active participation of stakeholders to greater or lesser degrees, depending on the context and

Evaluating, pages 59–71
Copyright © 2015 by Information Age Publishing
59

purpose of the study. In dialogue and deliberation, stakeholder views are tested against other views and against the available evidence. The legitimacy of the approach rests on fair, inclusive, and open procedures for deliberation, where discussion is not intimidated or manipulated (Stein, 2001).

The first principle is inclusion of relevant major interests. It doesn't seem right for evaluators to provide evaluations only for the highest bidders or most powerful stakeholders. That would bias evaluations towards special interests without due consideration of others. Nor would it be right to let sponsors of evaluations revise findings or change conclusions to advance their particular interests (Morris, 2011). Inclusion of all major interests is necessary. Otherwise, we would have stakeholder bias, which typically means bias in favor of the most powerful. Including all stakeholder views doesn't mean that evaluators should take all views at face value. No doubt some views are better founded than others, and evaluators have an obligation to respond to the quality of the arguments presented.

The second principle is dialogue. Evaluators should not presume to know how others think without engaging them in extensive dialogue. Too often, evaluators take the perspectives of the sponsors as definitive or presume they know how things stand. Too often, evaluators don't know when they think they do. A safeguard against such errors is to engage in dialogue with all stakeholders. This admonition comes from minority spokespeople and feminist philosophers, who have said repeatedly, "You only *think* you know what we think. You don't!" Again, evaluators need not take views uncritically. There should be ways of checking perspectives against other viewpoints and other evidence. However, evaluators should hear and understand all views first.

Another purpose of dialogue is to discover "real" interests. Evaluators shouldn't assume to know what the interests of the parties are nor take those interests as unchangeable. Through dialogue and deliberation, stakeholders may change their minds about their interests after they've considered other views. That's the point of discussion in a democracy. Of course, there is a legitimate concern that engaging in extensive dialogue will cause evaluators to be biased toward some stakeholders, perhaps be too sympathetic to developers or sponsors (Scriven, 1973). Certainly, that's a significant danger. However, being ignorant of stakeholder views and misunderstanding them are also significant dangers.

The third principle is deliberation. Deliberation is a cognitive process grounded in reasons, evidence, and valid arguments, including the methodological canons of evaluation. Here the special expertise of evaluators plays a particularly important role. Values are value claims (beliefs) that are subject to rational analysis and justification. Perspectives, values, and interests shouldn't be taken as fixed or unquestioned, but as subject to examination and revision through rational processes. Deliberation also requires that participants act in good faith and reason in ways that others will find acceptable. At the same time, participants should be open to revising their own views. Evaluators themselves are in a position to recognize and remedy biases and errors that plague evaluations in particular and thought processes in general. For example, one of the most common errors is that the conclusions of many evaluations don't match the data collected in the study, in my experience.

These three principles are straightforward, though not always easy to apply. Including all major stakeholders in the study, talking extensively with and among the groups, and spending considerable effort deliberating on the findings along with others can be blended with other evaluation approaches, designs, and methods since they require no particular research methods. Evaluators can democratize randomized studies, case studies, surveys, or any other approach. The key questions are which stakeholders are consulted and how they are included in the evaluation. Representation should be broad and extensive. What works in one place to facilitate involvement, dialogue, and deliberation might not work elsewhere. The limits to involving stakeholders are the resources available and the evaluator's ingenuity.

Biases Recognized by Cognitive Science

A major problem with our thinking processes is that we are inclined to construct simple stories that we take to be true, often based on little evidence (Kahneman, 2011). Such stories are simple, concrete, assign a large role to talent and intentions, and focus on a few striking events. Good stories provide a coherent account of people's intentions and actions, and we often fool ourselves that these stories are true when they're not. Since we can't help but deal with whatever evidence we have and base our stories on it, even when the evidence is sparse, we may have the illusion of understanding situations when we don't. As I emphasized in my validity book, coherence is an extremely powerful thinking disposition and a necessary one (House, 1980). Researchers of thought processes have confirmed this empirically.

One of Kahneman's examples is the over-emphasized role of CEOs of companies in analyzing corporate success. No doubt CEOs are important to companies, but the correlation between CEO quality and corporate success is .30 at best. Nonetheless, financial analysts regularly treat CEOs as if they alone are responsible for the success of the company. As a seasoned investor, I've learned to ignore interviews with CEOs when deciding which companies to invest in. From a research perspective, what's at work here is System 1's proclivity to jump to conclusions based on little evidence. Because of the powerful effect that Kahneman calls "what you see is all there is," only the evidence at hand counts, no matter how sparse that evidence may be. If investors don't have easily accessible information as to how good an investment in a stock is, they often substitute the question of how good the CEO appears to be, which is not the same thing.

Since System 1's main criterion for validity is coherence, we tend to have great subjective confidence in our stories and conclusions once they are constructed. This weakness in thinking applies to evaluators as well. When you enter an evaluation situation, you're looking for a coherent interpretation to make sense of things and tell you what to do. I've found that it's extremely difficult to keep your mind open to other possibilities. Within a short period of time, you think you understand what's going on. Keeping your mind open for an extended period requires determined effort.

The lesson here is that we need systematic checks on ourselves before jumping to conclusions, and we should take considerable effort to increase the diversity and amount of information that we take in. For example, it's easy to see how case study evaluators might base their evaluation on a few informants, especially those they like and agree with, and on other information that's limited in scope. Skimpy information may encourage them to construct a story that they themselves find compelling. The story may or may not be true. One can also imagine evaluation studies in which the criteria and measures are so narrowly drawn, though accurate in what they measure, that they result in narratives that are untrue, with the evaluators being certain their conclusions are correct because their numbers are correct.

I have noticed in myself that when I have told a story over and over many times, it grows truer in my mind with each retelling. Tentative confidence in the facts of the story the first time it was told tends to disappear as the story finds newer and appreciative audiences. Pretty soon the memory is of the telling of the story rather then the facts that created the story. It makes for good story telling, but not good truth telling.

To guard against these powerful biases, we need to extend the range of information that we collect. In fact, we should strive to discover discordant evidence that is contrary to what most people think. One way to do this is to engage a wide range of stakeholders who have diverse views, values, and interests so that we have a broad diverse picture of what's happening. In addition, we can collect different types of data to ensure that we haven't missed something critical. Democratizing evaluations encourages wide collection of information. For example, in the Denver project, I engaged a wide variety of stakeholders who provided different views about what was happening, different stories, as it were. I also collected different types of information, such as a checklist based on observations derived from school visits plus independent quantitative measures of program implementation. These two types of information were checks on each other. As a third check, we also solicited the opinions of the program staff members as to what they thought of our findings, a further challenge to our conclusions.

Insider Bias in Particular

In *Thinking Fast and Slow,* Kahneman tells several embarrassing stories about himself to illustrate his points. He says that one reason for his personal examples is that readers are far more likely to remember vivid personal stories, and these stories illustrate that researchers exhibit the same biases that they are researching. For example, when he was living in Israel, Kahneman developed a course to teach judgment and decision making to high school students. As he assembled a team to write a textbook for the course, he asked each participant on the team to estimate how long writing the book would take. The estimates centered around two years. He then asked the one curriculum expert in the group how long similar projects had taken curriculum developers in the past.

After some thought, the expert said that about 40% of the teams never finish, and of those that did finish, it took them from seven to ten years. Stunned at this estimate, Kahneman asked how his team compared to others in ability. "A little below average," the expert replied. Faced with contrary information that didn't fit their plans, Kahneman and his team simply ignored this information and proceeded with the project anyhow. They eventually finished the project eight years later! By the time the product was finished, the Ministry of Education had lost interest, and the textbook was never used. The team had failed to take into account the unforeseen disruptions that inevitably occur in projects, like divorces, illnesses, and bureaucratic delays. Their original estimate of two years was actually a best-case scenario, not a typical case.

Kahneman distinguishes two types of forecasting, the inside view and the outside view. The inside view is how the participants themselves see the world. The outside view is based on information collected about similar projects elsewhere. Even the one experienced curriculum developer on the development team, who had relevant outside information, estimated it would take the team only two years to complete the project. He ignored the class of events in which he was engaged. This is insider bias. A systematic way to mitigate this bias is to identify an appropriate reference class, obtain the statistics for this class of events, and use the typical case to generate baseline predictions. After that, you can use specific information about the particular case to adjust the baseline prediction. If the curriculum developers had done that, they would have correctly estimated the time required to write the text, or at least come much closer.

Sanna, Panter, Cohen, and Kennedy (2011) note similar biases and call them temporal or planning biases. These biases occur often in planning situations because planners inevitably predict much earlier completion dates than those actually realized. According to Sanna et al., unanticipated delays are major dangers in evaluations because evaluators often believe projects are much further along than they are and develop inappropriate expectations and measures of effectiveness. When projects don't meet the expectations or standards because they are slow in implementation, they're judged failures. That's what happened in the Denver evaluation. The implementation of the program was supposed to take two years. Six years later, it still wasn't fully implemented. Fortunately, I had anticipated this delay and structured the evaluation so the stakeholders could see the slow implementation and not assume the program was not being implemented at all. Evaluators also systematically underestimate how long their evaluations will take, thus frustrating sponsors and stakeholders. In the Denver project, we had many delays. Sanna et al. (2011) have specific suggestions about how evaluators might counter these biases.

Of course, such adjustments are difficult for people to make. Even cognitive researchers ignore important information. This is another area where evaluators can be useful. Evaluators can bring to bear their knowledge of the errors they and others are likely to make. They can do this by bringing outside views to bear. For example, in Denver, I gently suggested the current testing procedures might be unreliable to such an extent that the unreliability could mask the effects of the program. The school district conducted its own study to determine whether this was the case and changed their procedures. My estimates were based on prior knowledge about similar testing situations.

Another technique that Kahneman recommends is the *pre-mortem*, which he learned from Gary Klein. When a critical decision is about to be made, the idea is to gather the participant group together and say, "Imagine we are a year into the future. We implemented the project, and the outcome was a disaster. Write a brief history of that disaster." Such a procedure helps overcome the optimistic groupthink usually prevalent and stimulates the imagination about possible problems. It counters the suppression of doubt that feeds overconfidence. By being forced to reveal possible threats to the success, planners might be able to remedy the problems in advance.

What about the evaluator's own insider bias regarding the evaluation plan? I like the idea of having a personal guru outside the project with whom the evaluator can discuss the evaluation. The guru is someone with considerable experience and practical wisdom in evaluation, someone not afraid to raise questions that the evaluator might not have considered and who can offer advice and solutions. An outsider perspective can be invaluable, in addition to the perspectives already embedded in the DDE approach. I portray such an evaluator/guru relationship in my evaluation novel, *Regression to the Mean*, to be discussed in the practical wisdom part of this book (House, 2007).

Throughout this discussion, I've contended that evaluators are in the world, not outside it. In other words, they are subject to political pressures, conflicts of interest, overly optimistic estimates, and the same biases that other people are subject to. Evaluators are not immune to these influences. Unfortunately, evaluators sometimes tend to see themselves as outside the real world, in a kind of protected, buffered space where common biases and pressures do not affect them. In being unaware, they are vulnerable.

Caveats in Implementing the DDE Approach

Cultural Acceptability

There is no sense trying to conduct democratic evaluations in settings that are not democratic. It's difficult enough without having the underlying culture working against you. Democratic evaluation requires the foundation of a democratic culture. Even within democratic societies, there are significant differences. MacDonald's conception of democratic evaluation originated in the U.K. and did not fit easily into American culture. Karlsson's conception of democratic evaluation was developed in Sweden, one of the most democratic of societies, where stakeholder involvement in government enterprises is taken for granted. Some ideas may be too difficult to implement in other cultures. For example, Karlsson and Segerholm (2009) report trying to employ democratic procedures in Russia, only to discover that in Russian organizations, information not coming from the top down lacks any legitimacy. However, Mathison (2000) sees possibilities for conducting such democratic studies even in less than ideal circumstances. She may be right.

Cultural Divisions

Cultures themselves are not internally uniform. The Latino community in Denver consisted of the descendents of the Santa Fe culture, Chicanos, and recent immigrants, the latter mostly from rural Mexican villages. Among these groups there were differences in social class, values, and interests. The descendants of the Santa Fe culture had merged with Anglo culture over centuries. Members of this group held professional positions and ambitions to send their children to universities. The recent immigrants from Latin America were trying to survive economically. The Latino groups shared views and values (family, language, and religion), but also held some different values (education, career aspirations, and citizenship aspirations). Many immigrants wanted their children to learn English so they could quit school and get a job to help the family right away, an ambition opposed by school professionals. Many recent immigrants planned to return to their home country, not make a permanent home in the United States.

Faithful Representation

In Denver, lawyers represented the Latino community, but the lawyers themselves came from social classes and ethnic groups that were different from those of their clients. The lawyers had interests and views different from those they represented. As a practical matter, evaluators cannot involve all stakeholders directly. Faithful representation is a difficult issue in democratic evaluation and, indeed, in democracies generally.

Authentic Processes

There's a temptation for governments to pretend to want democratic involvement when they don't. Sometimes officials have already determined what the policies or programs will be and simply want to legitimate them with "pretend" participation. They hold public hearings, but the hearings are for show and have little influence on what the government has already determined. I would not attempt democratic evaluations in these circumstances.

Structured Interactions

Evaluations should be directed towards reaching evaluative conclusions. To be successful, interactions need structure. Discussions can't allow just anyone to express an opinion on any topic at any time or proceed in an undisciplined fashion. In trying to be open, there's a temptation to abandon rules and structures, letting people express their frustrations and feelings. However, evaluation is not therapy or counseling. Unbridled emoting and rambling digressions result in withdrawal by other participants who sense the process is going nowhere. For these reasons, large open public hearings are not usually productive. In Denver, there was a history of such meetings turning unruly, and I did not attempt to hold one, knowing the past history.

Issue Focused

Keeping everyone focused on specific issues is important. Bringing evidence, discussion, and joint deliberation to bear is a productive way of keeping things moving. It's not necessary that everyone like each other or agree on all matters. In fact, that's unlikely. What's useful is for participants to agree on the resolution of some specific issues. The process includes jointly determining what new evidence can be collected that will shed light on contested issues.

Rules

Evaluators need rules and procedures for dealing with culturally different people. The rules should not be too rigid; hopefully, they are adjusted to the people and the circumstances. On the other hand, evaluators shouldn't abandon all rules. Guidance is necessary. After all, deliberative democratic evaluation is democratic; it's not anarchic. Evaluators are operating within a democratic framework, not without a framework. There are necessary rules in democracies.

Transparency

In Denver it was critical that what we did was transparent so that we were not seen as taking sides or acting in our own interests. Transparency means that others do not have to guess what you are doing. That leaves less room for distrust and suspicions. At the same time, you can't do everything in a fishbowl. For example, I've been in situations where having spectators observe the meeting changes the discussion for the worse. Some discussants work to impress spectators rather than being engaged in the deliberations.

Sound Methods

It's worth remembering that evaluators have to produce good information. Evaluation hinges on good evidence and findings that are valid. That means good evaluation methods. It's no use discussing invalid findings.

Balance of Power

Power imbalances are threatening to democratic dialogues. They disrupt and distort discussion. The powerful may dominate discussions, and others may be intimidated, silenced, or disengaged. There should be a rough balance of power among participants for reasoned discussions to occur. If not, the evaluator needs procedures to balance things out.

Collaboration

The evaluator's role in deliberative democratic evaluation is one of collaboration, not capitulation. In Denver I had procedures for processing data and conducting deliberations. Even though I wanted to involve major stakeholders, I could not cede these procedures to the contending parties without affecting the honesty of the evaluation. We reached a critical juncture once when plaintiffs wanted us evaluators *not* to make holistic judgments but to give them the data and let them decide. I could see why they wanted to do this; they could decide if individual schools were in compliance. But if I had ceded this point, the monitoring project would have failed, in my view. I could see that eventually the two contending parties would be unlikely to agree on something they did not agree on now. To defend the point, I insisted we take the issue back to the judge and let him decide. I was ready to let the project go at that point. I suspected that the judge would recognize the necessity of the court monitor making these judgments impartially. And I suspect the plaintiffs realized the judge would be likely to see it that way too. They desisted.

Constraints on Self-Interests

Democratic processes work only if people do not act too excessively in their own self-interest. Democracies are undermined when everyone is grabbing what they can for themselves and manipulating democratic processes to obtain what they want. When this happens, the public interest is lost. Frankly, I don't know how to prevent this other than to promote a spirit that we are all in this together for our mutual advantage. If others don't see it that way and act selfishly, their behavior can ruin the democratic process. That's true in democratic governments, and it's true in democratic evaluations.

Modest Expectations

Democratic evaluation is no panacea. Indeed, no evaluation approach of any kind is a panacea. DDE is an approach that can have merit, particularly where strong partisan forces are operating, which we have a lot of in the United States. these days. (The checklist in the following appendix is to remind evaluators of various issues.)

Appendix

Deliberative Democratic Evaluation: A Checklist

The purpose of this checklist is to guide evaluations from a deliberative democratic perspective. Such evaluation incorporates democratic processes within the evaluation to secure better conclusions. The aspiration is to construct valid conclusions where there are conflicting views. The approach extends impartiality by including relevant interests, values, and views so that conclusions can be unbiased in value as well as factual aspects. Relevant value positions are included, but are subject to criticism the way other findings are. Not all value claims are equally defensible. The evaluator is still responsible for unbiased data collection, analysis, and arriving at sound conclusions. The guiding principles are inclusion, dialogue, and deliberation, which work in tandem with the professional canons of research validity.

Principle 1: Inclusion

The evaluation study should consider the interests, values, and views of major stakeholders involved in the program or policy under review. This does not mean that every interest, value, or view need be given equal weight, only that all relevant ones should be considered in the design and conduct of the evaluation.

Principle 2: Dialogue

The evaluation study should encourage extensive dialogue with stakeholder groups and sometimes dialogue among stakeholders. The aspiration is to prevent misunderstanding of interests, values, and views. However, the evaluator is under no obligation to accept views at face value. Nor does understanding entail agreement. The evaluator is responsible for structuring the dialogue.

Principle 3: Deliberation

The evaluation study should provide for extensive deliberation in arriving at conclusions. The aspiration is to draw well-considered conclusions. Sometimes stakeholders might participate in the deliberations to discover their true interests. The evaluator is responsible for structuring the deliberation and for the validity of the conclusions.

These three principles might be implemented by addressing specific questions. The questions may overlap each other, as might dialogue and deliberation processes. For example, some procedures that encourage dialogue might also promote deliberation.

1. Inclusion
   a. Whose interests are represented in the evaluation?
      – Specify the interests involved in the program and evaluation.
      – Identity relevant interests from the history of the program
      – Consider important interests that emerge from the cultural context.
   b. Are all major stakeholders represented?
      – Identify those interests not represented.
      – Seek ways of representing missing views.
      – Look for hidden commitments.
   c. Should some stakeholders be excluded?
      – Review the reasons for excluding some stakeholders.
      – Consider if representatives represent their groups authentically.
      – Clarify the evaluator's role in structuring the evaluation.

2. Dialogue
   a. Do power imbalances distort or impede dialogue and deliberation?
      – Examine the situation from the participants' point of view.
      – Consider whether participants will be forthcoming under the circumstances.
      – Consider whether some will exercise too much influence.
   b. Are there procedures to control power imbalances?
      – Do not take sides with factions.
      – Partition vociferous factions, if necessary.
      – Balance excessive self-interests.
   c. In what ways do stakeholders participate?
      – Secure commitments to rules and procedures in advance.
      – Structure the exchanges carefully around specific issues.
      – Structure forums suited to participant characteristics.
   d. How authentic is the participation?
      – Do not organize merely symbolic interactions.
      – Address the concerns put forth.
      – Secure the views of all stakeholders.
   e. How involved is the interaction?
      – Balance depth with breadth in participation.
      – Encourage receptivity to other views.
      – Insist on civil discourse.

3. Deliberation
   a. Is there reflective deliberation?
      – Organize resources for deliberation.
      – Clarify the roles of participants.

      – Have expertise play critical roles where relevant.

b. How extensive is the deliberation?

      – Review the main criteria.

      – Account for all the information.

      – Introduce important issues neglected by stakeholders.

c. How well considered is the deliberation?

      – Fit all the data together coherently.

      – Consider likely possibilities and reduce to best.

      – Draw the best conclusions for this context.

6

Underlying Values and Influences

What values and influences underlie the work of evaluators? In this chapter, I'll explore two questions. First, where did the conception of democratic evaluation come from? Second, what values and influences underlie the approach? Like most approaches, deliberative democratic evaluation is a blend and recombination of several streams of ideas over time. After all, creating new ideas is a reworking of old ones.

The democratic idea started with the values I learned in childhood from my family and community. I've discussed the importance of these sources of values earlier (Chapters 1 & 3). I also had several experiences as a teacher and teacher trainer that shaped my thinking about what was possible and desirable in education reform. These ideas played directly into how I thought evaluations of those reforms should be done. After my first evaluation, political and moral philosophy provided a framework for thinking about the political issues in evaluation, especially John Rawls's *A Theory of Justice* (1961), the premier political/moral work of the late twentieth century.

In the 1970s, Barry MacDonald from East Anglia and his idea of democratic evaluation influenced and reinforced my thinking about the politics

Evaluating, pages 73–83
Copyright © 2015 by Information Age Publishing
All rights of reproduction in any form reserved.

of evaluation. During the 1980s and 1990s, Ove Karlsson and several other Scandinavians provided ideas and concrete examples of how egalitarian societies can work. The contacts with Scandinavia bolstered my belief that egalitarian societies served their populations better and suggested possible directions for evaluation. During the 1990s, Ken Howe, my philosopher colleague, introduced me to minority and feminist critiques of Rawls's theory and to the deliberative democratic thinkers and their critiques of how the U.S. political structure was malfunctioning. By 1999, Howe and I had pulled these ideas together into deliberative democratic evaluation, named after the deliberative democratic thinkers (House & Howe, 1999). I'll discuss these influences in chronological order.

Family and Community

The place to start is where my values started, with my family and community, some of which I depicted earlier (Chapter 1). I came from an industrial working class family. At the end of the depression, we were poor. No one had a job. After my father was killed in a car accident, my sister and I lived on a tenant farm with an aunt and uncle for a few years, with no electricity or running water. We attended a one-room country school. During and after the war, heavy industry in the area boomed, generating jobs. My mother and second stepfather worked in a large munitions factory assembling blasting caps. One uncle burned the excess gunpowder at the plant, another sprayed poison gas at the local flourmill, and another worked for the teamsters union. Two uncles were alcoholics, what we now call street people. Although this was a time of relative affluence for this industrial community of Alton, Illinois, layoffs in the cyclical industrials were frequent; joblessness was always present. My mother and uncles expressed strong egalitarian, pro-union values, and I grew up embracing a strong egalitarian ethic.

In high school I was placed in the vocational track rather than with the college bound students. When I went to change my class schedule one day, the dean of boys looked at my standardized test scores and said, "House, what are you doing in there?" Actually, the counselors put everyone from my neighborhood into the vocational track. That's how the tracking system worked. In my sheet metal class at that time, we were making floats for the athletic director so he could jug fish on the Mississippi River, an illegal activity. I switched to the college bound courses for my last two years of high school. My mother had always wanted to be a teacher, but after her mother died, she had been forced to drop out of school in eighth grade to care for her family. She strongly encouraged me to go to college, and she saved five dollars from each paycheck to accumulate a college fund. In high school, a few key teachers lauded my writing skills and were important influences in prompting me on to college. Otherwise, I would have thought I didn't have the ability.

At nearby Washington University in St. Louis, I received a superb classic liberal education across a broad range of subjects, from the sciences and social sciences to ancient Greek history and philosophy. The university opened up a new world for me. I graduated Phi Beta Kappa, still holding to the egalitarian values of my family and social class. When I went back to visit my high school, my favorite teacher said that only about five students in the sixty-year history of the high school had done as well academically. Another said, "We didn't know you were that smart." I now had some intellectual resources to develop ideas.

Early Experiences as Teacher and Educator

Although I had an excellent opportunity to become a scholar in English literature, I wanted to do something more socially active, to change society. While deciding what to do, I took a job teaching high school. I had the usual problems learning the teaching craft until by my fourth year I was a reasonably good teacher. The University of Illinois was developing innovative teaching methods and materials, the "new" curricula, and I became involved as a teacher demonstrating the new techniques and materials to teachers visiting from other schools. The university invited me to join their project in Urbana to train and assist teachers around Illinois to implement the new curricula. From these experiences, I learned what can and cannot be done reforming education.

In general, the teacher culture, the school culture, and the parent culture work against school change. To change teaching behaviors, teachers have to be retrained, and this has to be done in teams so they can support one another when returning to their home district. Otherwise, the school culture will eradicate the new ideas. In addition, change must be strongly supported by principals. For lasting change to occur, teachers have to think and behave differently, and such changes can't be imposed forcibly from the outside. If they are, teachers subvert them. The most effective teacher training we did was "self-assessment," a form of evaluation. Under our guidance, teachers recorded and analyzed samples of their own classroom behavior with interaction schemes, and they practiced new behaviors with closely supervised feedback. Such change is effective, but time-consuming and expensive.

Unfortunately, in later decades federal and state authorities have attempted to force reform from the top down by requiring teachers to raise student achievement test scores, which are poor indicators of student learning. Teachers usually adjust by teaching what's on the tests. Such ill-considered reforms have made American education worse rather than better. Even after many decades of failure, the federal government continues to pursue the same strategy, regardless of which political party is in power. It's worth thinking about why governments continue to mandate the same strategies when they are clearly failures. (See Berliner, Glass, & Associates, 2014; Glass, 2008.)

John Rawls Theory of Justice

This teacher training led directly to a scholarship for graduate school. After finishing my degree, I conducted my first evaluation, a large, four-year evaluation of the Illinois Gifted Program for the state legislature, in fact, one of the first large evaluations in the country. Among other things, this experience made me realize that evaluation was permeated with politics. Was it all politics? It seemed to me that evaluators needed some way of navigating the politics rationally and ethically, instead of responding to pressures haphazardly or pretending that the politics were an anomaly.

In 1975, I read a review of Rawls theory of justice. I based my social justice position on Rawls work and introduced social justice as a criterion for evaluations. Rawls said that justice is the virtue of social institutions, and I envisioned evaluation as a developing social institution. At the time, the prevailing public theory of justice was utilitarianism, "the greatest good for the greatest number." In Rawls's analysis, the problem with utilitarianism was that it allowed trading off some people's rights and interests for those of others. For example, gross domestic product is considered a measure of economic progress. If problems arise in the economy, like inflation, it's permissible within the utilitarian framework to raise interest rates, which increases unemployment in order to control inflation. Of course, those at the lower end of the social scale are those forced to sacrifice for the general welfare, not those at the top.

Rawls proposed two principles of justice to mitigate such trade-offs. One principle assured every citizen of basic rights and liberties, similar to the U.S. Bill of Rights. The second principle limited inequality in society by maintaining that inequalities could be justified only if they benefitted the least advantaged. For example, it would be permissible to pay MDs high salaries if that benefits the poor. In short, Rawls theory is more egalitarian than utilitarianism. I suggested how Rawls's principles might be applied to evaluation. More generally, I argued that evaluators should be concerned about the disadvantaged members of society. At the time, this was a radical idea in evaluation.

Barry MacDonald and the British

In 1975, I spent several months with Barry MacDonald at the University of East Anglia on a Ford Foundation grant. MacDonald came from a working class background in Aberdeen, Scotland and was conducting case study evaluations as a member of the Humanities Curriculum Project. He agreed that evaluations were political and classified them into bureaucratic, autocratic, and democratic. In bureaucratic evaluations, evaluators accept the values of the office holders and have no independence. In autocratic evaluations, evaluators work from contractual agreements and conduct scientific evaluations that maintain the backing of their academic power base. In democratic evaluations, evaluators recognize value pluralism, seek to represent a range of interests in the evaluation, and work to inform the broader community. To some degree, MacDonald's ideas were shaped by his perception of the pervasive British class structure. Information was power, and it could be used for or against you. If you were lower in the social class structure, mostly it was used against. To mitigate this, MacDonald attempted to give some control of evaluation information to those from whom it was collected.

> Democratic evaluation is an information service to the community about the characteristics of an educational programme. It recognizes value-pluralism and seeks to represent a range of interests in its issue-formulation. The basic value is an informed citizenry, and the evaluator acts as broker in exchanges of information between differing groups. His techniques must be accessible to non-specialist audiences. His main activity is the collection of definitions of, and reactions to, the programme. He offers confidentiality to informants and gives them control over his use of information. The report is non-recommendatory, and the evaluator has no concept of information misuse. The evaluator engages in periodic negotiations of his relationships with sponsors and programme participants. The criterion of success is the range of audiences served. The report aspires to bestseller status. The key concepts are "confidentiality," "negotiation" and "accessibility." The key justificatory concept is 'the right to know.' (MacDonald, 1977, pp. 226–227)

Some of MacDonald's students and colleagues expanded on these ideas later (MacDonald & Kushner, 2004; Simons, 1987; Norris, 1990; Kushner, 2000).

My own position was that evaluators should act on Rawlsian principles of justice, whatever methods of evaluation they used. MacDonald had a specific method, case study, to conduct evaluations and suggested procedures for treating that information. Protecting participants was important. There were several aspects of MacDonald's evaluation that I liked, but other aspects didn't fit American culture very well. For example, refusing to draw conclusions and recommendations from a study was not workable in the United States, in my experience.

I had tried that in my first evaluation. I remember an assistant state superintendent of education pounding a long conference table with his fist, yelling at me, "We're paying you all this money to conduct this study and, damn it, we want some conclusions and recommendations! We'll decide what's worth doing!" I provided some conclusions. We were also having serious problems in the United States with evaluation findings being misused. In my view, evaluators had to be concerned about both the interpretation and use of findings. Otherwise powerful interest groups commandeered the findings and used them for their own purposes.

Although MacDonald's approach influenced and inspired me, I didn't employ it as such. I liked case studies as a way of getting close to the action, but I also wanted something that would apply to other methods as well. Overall, the egalitarian, democratic ethic was paramount in both our efforts, though manifested in different ways. Some of these differences reflected the different class structures in which we were operating. For the next several decades, we maintained close intellectual and personal contact until his death in 2013.

Ove Karlsson and the Scandinavians

In the 1980s and 1990s, Scandinavian scholars had a significant influence on my thinking. During those decades, I consulted with various groups in Sweden and Norway, culminating in service on an evaluation advisory board for Sigbrit Franke, Chancellor of the Swedish higher education system. These experiences introduced me to societies markedly more egalitarian than the United States and United Kingdom, and these societies seemed to function better. (International indicators of societal well-being on health, education, and income distribution, and the like, will reveal that the Scandanavian societies are near the top, while the United States is far down the list.) Ove Karlsson from Sweden and Peder Haug from Norway, both students of Ulf Lundgren, a prominent Swedish scholar, spent several months with me working on their dissertations about the politics of evaluation.

Scandinavian institutions and politics have a strong egalitarian ethos built into their operations. Ideas that would be controversial in the United States, such as having diverse interest groups participate in projects, are taken for granted there. The United States operates on a more elitist notion of democracy, one in which expert elites carry out what they take to be in the national interest. Nonetheless, I saw how well egalitarian societies could work and exchanged evaluation ideas with Karlsson, Haug, and others.

For his dissertation, Karlsson (1996) conducted an evaluation that illustrates extensive involvement, dialogue, and deliberation. He evaluated a program providing care and leisure services for school-age children ages 9–12. The program aimed for efficient organization of such services and new pedagogical content to be achieved through School Age Care Centers. Politicians wanted to know how such services could be organized, with what pedagogical content, what the centers would cost, and what children and parents wanted the centers to be.

Karlsson's first step was to identify stakeholder groups and choose representatives from them, including politicians, managers, professionals, parents, and children. He surveyed parents and interviewed stakeholder groups on certain issues:

Politicians—What is the aim of the program?
Management—What is required to manage such a program?
Cooperating professionals—What expectations are there from others who work in this field?
Staff union—What do staff unions require?
Parents—What do parents want the program to be?
Children—What expectations do the children have?

Data were communicated to stakeholders in the form of four metaphors of ideal types of school age care center. The metaphors were the workshop, the classroom, the coffee bar, and the living room. The second stage focused on implementation, 25 centers serving 500 students. The evaluators used a "bottom-up" approach by asking children how they experienced the centers, as opposed to the "top-down" approach of the first stage. Next, parents and cooperating professionals, then managers and politicians, were interviewed. Dialogue was achieved by presenting to later groups what the prior groups had said. In the first two stages the dialogue admitted distance and space among participants so they could talk more freely.

In the third stage the goal was face-to-face dialogue and establishing mutual and reciprocal relationships. The aim was to develop genuine and critical dialogue that could stimulate new thoughts among stakeholders and bring conflicts into open discussion. Four meetings were arranged. To ensure that everyone could have a say, four professional actors played short scenes illustrating critical questions and conflicts. The actors involved the audiences in dialogues through scenarios showing the essence of problems (identified from the data) and enlisting audiences to help the actors solve or develop new ways to see the problems.

In Karlsson's view, the aim of critical dialogues is to develop a deeper understanding of the program. The important aim is to enable the powerless to have influence. The evaluator has two responsibilities: developing a theoretical perspective and cultivating critical inquiry. "Theoretical perspective" means developing a framework that puts the program in historical and political context for participants (Haug, 1996). In Karlsson's view, the difficulty with dialogue as a strategy is that it demands that every interest group have enough resources to participate. There's a risk of participation by only those who are resource rich. The overall Scandinavian influence on my own approach is strong.

Ken Howe and the Deliberative Democratic Thinkers

In the 1990s, my philosopher colleague Ken Howe introduced me to critiques of Rawls and to the deliberative democratic thinkers. The latter are mostly political scientists and philosophers who contend that democratic processes in the United States are seriously flawed. Governing processes are dominated by elites who do not represent the interests of the general population. Because of this, government is losing its legitimacy. These critics suggest broader participation by citizens in policy processes so that their interests can be represented directly.

Advocates label this approach deliberative democracy (e.g., Fishkin, 1991; Gutmann & Thompson, 1996, 2004; Elster, 1998; Dryzek, 2000).

> ...we can define deliberative democracy as a form of government in which free and equal citizens (and their representatives) justify decisions in a process in which they give one another reasons that are mutually acceptable and generally accessible, with the aim of reaching conclusions that are binding in the present on all citizens but open to challenge in the future. (Gutmann & Thompson, 2004, p. 7)

The focus is on reasoning with each other.

> Increasingly, democratic legitimacy came to be seen in terms of the ability or opportunity to participate in effective deliberation on the part of those subject to collective decisions.... The reflection aspect is critical, because reference can be transformed in the process of deliberation. Deliberation as a social process is distinguished from other kinds of communication in that deliberators are amenable to changing their judgments, preferences, and views during the course of their interactions, which involve persuasion rather than coercion, manipulation, or deception.... The deliberative turn represents a renewed concern with the authenticity of democracy.... (Dryzek, 2000, p. 1)

By 1999, Howe and I had encapsulated all these influences in our conception of deliberative democratic evaluation, part of a broader analysis of the role of values in evaluation (House & Howe, 1999). Howe came from a Flint, Michigan industrial working class background similar to mine. Before attending the university, he worked in a Buick plant and as a house painter. Later, in his philosophy training, he embraced pragmatism, where John Dewey's influence was still strong.

Dewey advocated social problem solving that included members of the public in social inquiry. In fact, some have called Dewey the first deliberative democratic theorist. In his time, Dewey thought that the public interest was not being addressed adequately. His judgment of governing by expert elites was this: "A class of experts is inevitably so removed from common interests as to become a class with private interests and private knowledge, which is in social matters is no knowledge at all" (Dewey, 1927, 19, location 2927). "No government by experts in which the masses do not have a chance to inform the experts as to their needs can be anything but an oligarchy managed in the interests of the few" (Dewey, 1927, l. 476.)

To my surprise, when Lee Cronbach introduced me as a speaker at Stake's retirement symposium, Cronbach said he was already familiar with the deliberative democratic evaluation ideas I was presenting since he and Tom Hastings, the founder of our evaluation center at Illinois, had been students together at the University of Chicago when Dewey was there! In fact, Cronbach's *Towards Reform of Program Evaluation* (1980), which focuses on politics, was quite compatible with such ideas. Such is the churn and return of ideas.

A noteworthy theme throughout this chapter is the strong influence of social class. Several scholars who influenced me personally, MacDonald, Karlsson, and Howe, came from working class backgrounds, albeit from different countries, each with somewhat different class structures. They were all concerned about the welfare of the powerless and the poor. Why? Possibly because they had experienced the effects of being poor and powerless firsthand. They knew what damage could be done. If you grow up in the working class, you see what it means to be out of work for a long time, not to be able to provide for your family, and not to be able to afford medicine or education. These experiences are vivid. As the cognitive researchers note, it's the vivid experiences that prompt people to action.

What about the influence of other evaluators on my thinking? At the beginning of my career, I was strongly influenced by Stake and Scriven, who often disagreed with each other, as I've noted elsewhere (Chapter 2 and in House, 2013). Stake followed the case study approach, strongly influenced by MacDonald, which featured close contact with program participants and representing those views in case studies. Initially, Stake saw these studies as being "subjective," though he has changed his position about this from time to time.

On the other hand, Scriven saw evaluations as being objective—discussed earlier (Chapter 3)—and he advocated using evaluation methods to reduce biases. I combined both Stake's and Scriven's views in deliberative democratic evaluation by turning them around. I followed the practice of including the views of participants in evaluations; but by combining stakeholder views, values, and interests, I asserted that evaluators could arrive at conclusions that were objective. By objective I meant Scriven's notion of "without bias." If you include the views of only a few stakeholders, like sponsors, you risk stakeholder bias. Broad inclusion protects against the epistemic biases recognized by cognitive research and against overconfidence (Scriven, 1973; Stake, 1967, 1978).

Reprise

Hence, the DDE approach was derived from family and community, from first hand experiences with evaluation politics, from evaluation theory, from philosophy and political science, from British influence, MacDonald being the first to use the term democratic evaluation; from Scandinavian influences, and from the deliberative democratic thinkers, first to use the deliberative democracy term. Other evaluators have presented compatible ideas from their own perspectives, including Karlsson (1996, 2003), Segerholm (2003), Hanberger (2001), Murray (2002) in Sweden, Krogstrup (2003) in Denmark, and Monsen in Norway. In the US, Greene (1997, 2000, 2003, 2013), Mathison (2000), Schwandt (2003), King (1998), Ryan (Ryan & DeStefano, 2000), Mark, Henry, and Julnes (2000), Hood, Hopson, and Frierson (2005), and Patton (2002) have addressed similar issues.

Ultimately, the core values underlying this approach are democratic egalitarianism, manifested in democratic concepts and procedures, and epistemic values recognized by cognitive researchers, what Stanovich calls "reflectivity," perhaps more commonly known as critical thinking. The underlying core values are both moral and epistemic. Inclusion, dialogue, and deliberation try to accomplish both.

With deliberative democratic evaluation, we arrive at the idea of a group of evaluators and stakeholders representing a wide range of interests, including the poor and powerless, discussing and deliberating together about the evaluation study and its findings. As noted earlier, the basic source of knowledge is interpersonal communication. Indeed, a community of minds is the basis for all knowledge and provides the meaning of things. Participants engaged in interpersonal communication can generate ideas and provide checks on the meaning of concepts. As a local community of interest, the evaluation group generates knowledge about a program by integrating knowledge from its members with that from evaluation methods. Idealistic? Yes, no doubt. Impossible? No, at least no more impossible than democracy itself.

Footnote: Democracy and Capitalism

In editing this book, Jennifer Greene raised the issue as to how the investing incident I described in Chapter 1 relates to the strong egalitarian values I endorse. I'm addressing the interaction between democracy and capitalism in work elsewhere, but I'll indicate the direction of my thoughts. First, we live an explicitly capitalist democracy in which economic behavior is structured in particular ways. For example, if you want to have money for retirement, you must invest in a retirement scheme. Every retirement operation in the country invests in the financial and property markets, all of them capitalist enterprises. The single exception is federal social security, which takes in money from paychecks and promises to repay its recipients from federal revenues later in their lives. Social security is based on a promise, not an investment.

As an individual you have little choice but to play by the established rules for retirement. You have to balance your sense of social justice with your retirement needs and the many other things you value, such as current consumption, your children's education, and health expenses for you and your family. In any life, no single value can be maximized; all values must be balanced against others. Otherwise, unless you inherit money, almost certain to be the product of other capitalist enterprises, you will have no retirement money. Of course, this analysis assumes a socially just system, which Americans have been assured they have. The basic argument is that the capitalist system produces more economically and redistributes income so that everyone is better off with than without capitalism.

But what if the economic system is not economically just? There is mounting evidence that inequality in the United States has reached an extreme not seen since the beginning of the twentieth century. If this is the case, individuals have a right and an obligation to try to change the system and the rules by which income and wealth are distributed. The current system certainly looks unjust to many. However, individuals can't simply decide one day to live by a different set of rules of their own making. Until they are changed, the old rules still apply. I would also suggest that evaluators as a profession need to examine the issue of economic inequality to see whether there is a role for the profession in rectifying extreme inequality, assuming that the system has indeed become unjust. In fact, I would suggest that there is such a role.

PART III

Practical Wisdom in Evaluation

Most evaluators believe that knowledge derived from experience is valuable when we conduct evaluations. We call this expertise practical knowledge, clinical knowledge, or practical wisdom. I prefer the term practical wisdom because I think the knowledge gained from experience is quite valuable and influential. Tom Schwandt (2003, 2005, 2008), in particular, has stressed the importance of practical wisdom in evaluation. In the third part of this book, I address three questions. What is practical wisdom? How do we learn it? How valid is it? Providing examples of practical wisdom is difficult because such knowledge is highly contextual and manifested only in specific situations.

In Chapter 7, I specify situations in the Denver project where I drew upon practical knowledge based on my prior experiences. This knowledge varied from knowing how school districts use standardized tests, to how new student data systems are likely to be long delayed in operation, to how education programs take longer to implement than anyone expects. I tie these examples to how I conducted the Denver evaluation. I also note how my practical knowledge in handling some situations was inadequate. For example, I did not do a good job of informing the general public about the findings of my evaluation.

Evaluating, pages 85–86
Copyright © 2015 by Information Age Publishing

In Chapter 8, I use scenes from my evaluation novel to illustrate practical wisdom at work (House, 2007). I describe how and why I wrote the novel about evaluation. The novel illustrates several lessons, particularly about the politics and ethics, topics not easy to analyze. I adapted a technique used by the late movie critic Roger Ebert. Ebert analyzed movies by playing a classic like *Casablanca* before an audience and stopping the movie on a scene when someone in the audience yelled, "Stop." Ebert would explain in astonishing detail precisely what was happening in that particular scene. Similarly, I've presented scenes from the novel and explained what lies behind them, unfortunately without the same talent Ebert possessed.

Using the same technique, in Chapter 9, I discuss whether practical wisdom based on experience is valid. Based on the research about clinical expertise, Kahneman has never been positive about the validity of clinical knowledge. However, after a careful review of different fields, he has specified the conditions under which practical knowledge can be valid in a given field. Fortunately, I believe evaluation as a field meets the criteria for the validity of practical knowledge. Finally, in the last section, I arrive at a set of general conclusions that might be derived from the book as a whole.

7

Evaluating With Practical Wisdom

Anyone who has conducted an evaluation knows that there's the way you intended to do the study and then the way you actually did the study. Usually, something happens that throws you off course and forces you to think, "Now what? What do I do?" How well you can handle disruptive events involves what some people call practical wisdom or practical knowledge. Being a good evaluator doesn't depend solely on plans and methods. It also depends on practical wisdom learned mostly through on-the-job experiences, both good and bad.

In their book *Practical Wisdom*, Barry Schwartz and Kenneth Sharpe (2010) tell the story of Luke, a custodian working at a large teaching hospital. A young comatose man was a patient in one of Luke's rooms. The man had gotten into a fight in a bar and had been seriously injured. He hadn't gained consciousness for six months and showed no signs of doing so. During this period, his father spent a huge amount of time at his son's bedside, hoping for a miracle. One day, while the father was out smoking a cigarette, Luke cleaned the room. When the father came back, he became angry and accused Luke of not having cleaned. At first Luke started to argue with him,

Evaluating, pages 87–97

but then decided that wasn't the wisest course of action. Luke cleaned the room again with the father watching him do it.

In Schwartz and Sharpe's judgment, this is an excellent example of practical wisdom, of doing what makes the situation better, instead of merely doing what's in the job description. Luke could have argued with the father, insisting that he had already cleaned the room and trying to demonstrate that to him. But Luke thought about what the father had been through emotionally and how distraught the man was. What good would arguing with him do? Instead, Luke cleaned the room again, possibly making the man feel that he had done something worthwhile for his son, no matter how small, and no matter how far out of reach the son was. Luke not only did the humanitarian thing, something no one else would know or appreciate, he did the practically wise thing.

Of course, none of this was in Luke's job description. However, the researchers who collected this information discovered that many custodians at the hospital had defined their jobs in such a way that "care giving" was an important part of the job they were doing. Custodians often did things that would improve the welfare of their patients, well beyond janitorial duties. No one told them to do these things; it was something they offered on their own, beyond the specified tasks of the job.

In Schwartz and Sharpe's view, this is an example of what Aristotle called practical wisdom. Aristotle developed the idea by watching blacksmiths, carpenters, shoemakers, boat pilots, and other craftsmen around Athens apply their skills. The workmen didn't have rigid rules they followed. The materials they worked with and the tasks they performed were too varied and irregular for that. New contexts posed new problems. For example, when stonemasons had to carve rounded columns, they took a flat ruler and changed it to a flexible one that could measure the curved surfaces they worked on, in a literal sense "bending the rules." Aristotle thought that practical wisdom consisted of such actions taken in particular work contexts.

Practical wisdom consists of doing the right thing in the special circumstances of performing the job. Professional practices, including evaluation, also require such choices. What do you do in difficult situations? The wisdom to address such questions is practical. It depends on your ability to perceive the situation, have the appropriate feelings about it, deliberate about what's appropriate in these circumstances, and, finally, to act. Practical wisdom requires learned character traits like self-control and self-knowledge. It involves making choices among desirable outcomes that conflict with one other or choosing between the better and best possibilities. These choices require nuanced practical judgments appropriate to the time and circumstances.

The person in evaluation who has written most eloquently about professional practice and practical knowledge is Tom Schwandt (2008, 2005, 2003). In several articles and books, he has emphasized the centrality of practice to our evaluations. In his view, any professional practice is a complicated network of transactions in which practitioner judgments are tested repeatedly. There is no way to avoid these complex social interactions.

> Our everyday practice as teachers, managers, social service workers, and health care providers tells us that no escape from these dilemmas can be found. We are, as I have argued elsewhere, always on the "rough ground" where values, personalities, evidence, information, feelings, sensitivities, emotions, affect, ambiguities, contradictions, inconsistencies, and so forth are simultaneously in play as we try to do the right thing and do it well. (Schwandt, 2005, p. 99)

That says it pretty well for the practice of evaluators.

Schwartz and Sharpe say the practically wise person:

- Is guided by the overall aims of the activity
- Knows how to improvise, to balance conflicting aims, and to interpret rules in light of the particulars of the context
- Is socially perceptive and knows how to interpret the social context
- Knows how to understand the perspectives of other people, to see the situation as another person might see it, and to know how the other person feels
- Knows how to make emotion an ally of reason and to rely on emotions to signal what's called for
- Is highly experienced: practical wisdom is based on a lot of experience

For example, Luke framed the issue as one of how to care for and sustain the relationship of father and son at this particular time, not one of simply cleaning the room. He framed the situation through his understanding of what had happened and what was happening emotionally between father and son. He knew their story and attended to it. He also knew that the men with whom the son had been fighting were African Americans, as was Luke. He considered what courses of action were possible in the circumstances. The story framed the issue in such a way that it enabled Luke to figure out what to do. No doubt his ability to construct such a narrative was based on the type of person Luke was, his character, as well as on his prior experiences in the hospital. No doubt the type of person Luke was had been influenced by his experiences in the hospital.

The ability to construct appropriate stories and frame situations with them is critical to practical moral skill. So too is the ability to use analogies and metaphors to draw on past experiences. Luke remembered the consequences of similar actions he had taken in past. Perhaps he had argued with someone in a similar situation and had seen that the consequences of that argument helped no one. Learning from experience often means learning from the consequences of bad experiences where you didn't make the wisest choice. Figuring out what's appropriate also requires moral perception and empathy. Luke had to perceive what the father must be feeling and thinking. Finally, and importantly, not only did Luke perceive the situation, he was motivated to act on his perception. Acting at the right time is part of practical wisdom.

From this incident Luke seems to be a compassionate man able and willing to perceive things, including emotions of other people, and willing to act on these perceptions. I doubt that I would have risen to such an occasion. Based on my own character, I suspect I would have been more likely to argue with the father, not so much because I couldn't see his plight, as having the tendency to push back when someone accuses me of something I didn't do. I think I would have argued first and regretted it later when I thought it over. My character is less compassionate than that of Luke. Stepping back from the event, I can see how Luke's actions were superior to what I might have done.

A substantial part of moral imagination is the ability to see how various options will play out. Empathy is critical in this assessment, including discerning what others are thinking and feeling. Emotion is also critical as a signaling device. Luke could see how angry the father was and knew that the father's anger wasn't simply about cleaning the room. It was about the entire unfortunate tragedy. Luke, in turn, had to manage his own emotions skillfully. Surely, he must have felt a surge of anger when the father lashed out at him unjustifiably. Luke had to assess and discipline his own feelings and reactions. He didn't get defensive, at least not after his immediate reaction.

Practical wisdom is not about establishing rules and following them. It's about if, when, and how to apply the rules. It's context dependent and operates in areas of gray, not black and white. By themselves, rules tend to marginalize the importance of character traits like compassion, empathy, courage, patience, and kindness. You learn rules from books and teachers. You learn practical wisdom from experience, coaches, and mentors.

In this sense, we must admire the hospital where this incident occurred. Apparently, Luke was not the only one who attended to the welfare of patients and included that task in their job performance. According to the researchers, other custodians did similar things for their patients. Somehow an *esprit* was built into the culture of the institution. I don't need to provide negative examples of health care institutions where patients' welfare is not a high aim or concern. Readers can supply many negative examples of their own. We should commend institutions able to nurture such values and character traits in their staffs. And we should aspire to this level of understanding and action in the evaluation profession. After all, like the medical profession, evaluation has the capacity to inflict considerable damage if uncaring.

What are some other components of practical wisdom? We can profit from the research on thinking, discussed earlier (Chapter 2). Cognitive components include "fuzzy" concepts, frames, stories, pattern recognition, and intuitive thinking. Fuzzy concepts are not clearly defined as mathematical concepts are. The concept of fruit is a good example. The natural category of fruit has graded membership. Some fruits are core examples of the concept, while others have fewer degrees of membership. Humans have great capacity to handle fuzzy concepts like this, and this fuzziness allows them to make nuanced judgments in different contexts based on fuzzy concepts.

For example, if a judge and jury must make a careful determination about whether an act is an "armed robbery," their considered judgment depends very much on the particulars of the context. The fate of the defendant may depend greatly on what the jury determines. According to researchers, we think with such fuzzy ideas. And fuzzy concepts include those like "inclusion," dialogue," and "deliberation" discussed earlier. When to apply and balance concepts like these and how to apply guidelines like "include stakeholders in the evaluation" requires interpretation in context. There are no hard and fast rules for doing so. Practical wisdom improves with experience.

Another critical element of practical wisdom is framing. Frames tell us what's important, and what to compare, and they help us discern what's relevant in a particular context. All humans have the capacity to frame, which allows them to interpret events. Of course, the wrong frames can also bias and distort. For example, negative uses might include political spinning of events. There is no neutral frame-free way to interpret or evaluate anything. The problem is to choose the right frame.

For example, Luke could have framed his situation as one of strict job performance. He could have told the father that he had cleaned the room and pointed to signs that he did. Or he could have framed the situation as protecting his job. He could have gone straight to his supervisor. What if the father told Luke's supervisor that Luke had failed to clean the room? Luke's job might be in jeopardy. Instead, Luke took the nobler view by framing the situation with a narrative about where the father and son stood at this moment in their lives and acted humanely. Stories and narratives are powerful ways that we frame and understand lives, including our own, as well as what we should do. They depend on values, character, and experience.

Such thinking also includes pattern recognition. When people become expert at performing a task, they recognize patterns and combinations of patterns they've seen before. They've learned these patterns through experience, including bad experiences. Learning depends on the community, watching others, and making decisions. Of course, some decisions require careful deliberation and slow thinking, especially when moral perception is conflicted or unclear. I would put Luke's behavior in that category. In Luke's case, his thinking involved a carefully considered balancing of different actions, not a quick automatic response. With his experience, it may have invoked a familiar pattern that enabled him to respond quickly. I must say that it's not an experience or pattern that I have in my own repertoire, though I can appreciate it on reflection.

Practical Wisdom in Denver

How might these ideas play out in evaluations? For example, what knowledge and experience lay behind decisions that I made in the Denver evaluation? Overall, I was applying evaluation methods as well as the fuzzy guidelines of inclusion, dialogue, and deliberation. I used practical knowledge gained from more than three decades of conducting evaluations. Below are situations where past experiences guided what I did. In some situations, I succeeded and in some I failed. Even with decades of evaluation experience, my practical knowledge wasn't always equal to the task.

The Extremely Politicized Situation

The Denver bilingual program had been in the news for many years. The court case had started as desegregation litigation and evolved into a language case. The plaintiffs had gone back to federal court and renegotiated a language instruction program for students who could not speak English well enough to be in regular classes. During these years, antagonisms between the school district and Latino community had become intense.

I set up my first meeting with the Denver superintendent of schools. That meeting turned out to be quite rough. The superintendent wanted me to act as total arbiter of the new court agreement. One option was to assume the legal authority of the court and declare "what was what." However, in thinking about the politics, I decided to be more conciliatory and inclusive. I had been involved in several politicized evaluations before, and my sense of how things worked out was that the long-term results would be better if you listened to other people, tried to understand their point of view, tried to address their concerns, and tired to reconcile differences. At the same time, I had also learned that you can't let others run over top of you or you would lose control of the evaluation. If you lose control, the most powerful stakeholders win, whoever they may be and whatever the issues. I struck a balance between using my authority and sharing it with stakeholders. And this required balanced judgment.

I also decided to be open about what I was doing, with the idea of building a sense of trust and credibility. The first superintendent didn't like that. He thought that the Latinos would never accept those conditions and would take advantage of them for their own political purposes. I wasn't sure how things would work out either, but I was piecing together an approach based on intuitions from previous rough and tumble evaluations. To his credit, the superintendent accepted my approach, even though he disagreed with it.

New Data System Not Working

Some practical knowledge is based on particular experiences. I built the monitoring plan around the new data system the school district was implementing. The district had contracted for the development of the data system to an outside group. My plan was to collect quantitative data on a few key indicators in each school. Where I saw schools showing poor performance on the implementation indicators, my plan was to send in a team to ascertain what the problems were. We could then find solutions for the problem schools. Employing the data system that way meant that we would not have to visit every school.

Unfortunately, the outside data contractors were having all kinds of technical problems merging files and the like. In short, the data system wasn't usable. Relying on what the contractors told them, the district said the new system would be ready shortly. Based on my previous experiences with installing new technologies, I was skeptical. One of my early evaluations was of the PLATO teaching and learning system at the University of Illinois in the early 1970s. This was one of the first computer-assisted learning attempts, and it relied on terminals in the Chicago Community Colleges hooked up to mainframe computers on the Urbana campus.

The whole system was ingenious technically, one of the first uses of touch screens. However, not even the high-powered engineers at the university could keep the physical equipment working long enough for community college instructors to use the system. The instructors would try the terminals a few times, and if they didn't work, they would quit altogether. They had too many other things to do to spend time messing around with non-functioning equipment. I knew that implementing new data systems usually encountered long delays and many unseen problems, even in universities.

What should I do? I anticipated that the data system might take a couple of years to become functional (which turned out to be accurate). Should I wait two years and do nothing? The non-functioning data system wasn't my fault, and no one would blame me, but here was the federal court, the city, and the schools wanting information about whether this controversial program was being implemented. Such a delay seemed unacceptable, whatever the cause. I could endanger the entire project by delaying action.

Another possibility was to send questionnaires to the schools. However, I was reluctant to do that. In evaluating the Illinois Gifted Education program thirty years before (my first evaluation), I mailed questionnaires to a thousand schools in Illinois to provide quick information for the Illinois legislature. I discovered later that the information I received was highly suspect. For example, the questionnaires to the Chicago high schools came back all in one package, filled out in the same handwriting, tied together with a ribbon. According to the answers, every Chicago high school was providing every desirable option for academically talented children. I knew from previous experience that I could spend months running up and down the halls of school district headquarters at LaSalle Street without straightening out the data. Since that time, I've been highly suspicious of self-report questionnaires when respondents have something to lose, or think they do.

Another alternative was to visit all the schools in the program over the next few years, using a checklist based on the court agreement. That meant a labor-intensive approach. The approach was inefficient, but I didn't see a better choice. I had wanted quantitative indicators from centralized data systems because they would be more credible to all parties than relying on checklist visits conducted in a politicized atmosphere. However, given the circumstances, it would have to be the other way around, with the checklist visits backed by indicators from the data system eventually. To bolster the credibility of the checklist approach, I enlisted the help of the major stakeholders in constructing the checklist and sought their approval all along the way. As it turned out, the checklist worked pretty well. (Actually, such simple checklists can be valid and useful if handled properly. See Kahneman, 2011, Chapter 21, and Scriven's work on checklists.)

Selecting Evaluation Staff to Help

Once I had decided on using visits with a checklist to collect the initial data, I needed someone to help me to do so. As discussed earlier, the choices were to use graduate students or else someone connected to the program and school district. I knew from past experience that large institutions like schools find it easy to hide whatever they want to hide. Outsiders are at a severe disadvantage when they visit schools to elicit information. I had been a teacher and understood how schools work. School personnel are extremely reluctant to reveal negative information that might make their school or district look bad. They feel vulnerable, and, in fact, they are highly vulnerable to public opinion.

If I used graduate students to collect data, they would have a difficult time collecting sensitive information. This wasn't a matter of technique, but of knowing how the system operates and knowing the people in it. If you're a teacher, why reveal negative information about your program to a group of people you don't know? Better to protect the program and (in your view) the students. Consequently, I decided to use two retired principals as data collectors. Both were Latinas, and both had been strong ELA program supporters in the district. My reasoning was that they knew how the district and program operated and that people in the program would be more likely to tell them the truth about what was going on. Their former colleagues would figure the former principals were not trying to damage the program.

I also tried to vet a former teacher/administrator whom I knew would be first rate in helping with the evaluation. However, the district was not keen on her since she had been so militant in the past. When I submitted her name, the district response was something like this, "Well, as court monitor you have the authority to appoint whomever you want as a data collector, but why pick her, given her past militant record, when it will diminish the credibility of your findings with us?" Reluctantly, I withdrew her name.

Using the former principals did raise the issue of potential bias and their lack of training as data collectors. To combat this, I instituted safeguards to control for biases. To help my colleagues separate their opinions from the monitoring, I added a section at the end of the checklist where they provided their professional opinions, with the understanding that these particular comments did not have to be based on criteria from the legal agreement. This section gave them an outlet to register insights derived from their expertise. The opinion section helped them (and me) sort out their judgments from other (often invaluable) insights. They felt better because they were able to report what they considered important information, and their insights did not go unrecorded or unrecognized. (Again, see Kahneman, 2011, Chapter 21.)

The Unreliability of Testing

The bilingual program depended heavily on testing students who were deficient in English to gain entry into the program and testing them again to move them to regular classes. Many staff members around the district administered the tests. The testing required training to be done properly. I figured the testing procedures would produce highly variable results. In other words, the testing was not reliable with minimal training for so many different testers. I didn't say anything about this at the beginning of the monitoring since we had other things to do.

I waited until we began obtaining some peculiar results in the data. I suggested that one possible source of the peculiarities might be unreliable administering of the tests. Rather than claim that it was so, I suggested the district run its own study. The assistant superintendent was quite competent and conducted a small study, revealing that the testing was unreliable. Of course, we weren't seeking the testing reliability that one would secure for a published study. But the results were so far off that the district personnel could see that the unreliability could make the program look ineffective. Consequently, the district reduced the number of testers and instituted retraining for those remaining.

Personalities

Obviously, when you have a group of people working closely together on a difficult and politicized endeavor, the interaction of particular personalities can be interesting. To discuss the personalities of others involved in this evaluation seems to me to violate their privacy. In an earlier chapter, I've discussed my own personality and how it influenced my work. How did it affect this evaluation? First, the evaluation was a highly politicized evaluation that had considerable import for poor and disadvantaged people. Projects helping the poor and the powerless are high on my personal agenda, given the circumstances of my own background. I want those programs to work, and if they don't work, I want to know that too. I don't do disadvantaged students any favors by inflicting programs on them that don't help them. I presumed that the others involved in the project had similar motivations, though we didn't always agree on every issue.

Failure: Informing the Public

The examples so far have been success stories where I came up with ideas about how to manage puzzling situations. It's worth noting a few failures where I did not possess the practical knowledge necessary to succeed. One instance was informing the general public. I wrote progress reports every several months and submitted those to the federal court. As part of the court procedures, the reports became public knowledge. Reporters read the reports and had many questions for me.

I asked the parties how I should respond. Both sides had a previously contentious relationship with the media, and both advised me not to answer questions. When reporters called, I referred them to the district and the plaintiffs for their interpretation of the reports. This wasn't entirely satisfactory because both sides gave their own interpretations. I never came up with a better idea for how I should have involved the public, and I still don't know. That's knowledge I don't have.

Failure: Convincing Some Lawyers

Another failure was my inability to convince at least one lawyer that the district was not failing to select some students that should be in the program. I went through student files several times to look at how many students were not selected who should be. For some reason, the lawyer remained convinced that the schools had secret files showing that certain students had been excluded. He suggested that we search through schools to find these secret files.

I had no idea what he was talking about. This was not part of any school procedures, as I knew them. I asked my colleagues, the former principals, if they had heard of such secret files. They hadn't. I didn't know what to do to persuade him that the error rate was as we said it was, based on the central office files. It did occur to me that maybe there was no way to persuade him. Maybe he was being "lawyerly," holding a position for his clients in case they wanted grounds on which to challenge the overall monitoring results later. Dealing with lawyers is not quite like dealing with other people. Fortunately, we agreed on most of the data that we collected during the monitoring.

There's no doubt that my previous experience in evaluation over many years alerted me to problems and how to deal with them that I wouldn't have had if this were my first evaluation. I also think I treated people better and worked with them better as a result of being involved in many evaluations. The idea of practical wisdom makes a good deal of sense as a case of having the right values and information and being able to frame issues in the best way. And this isn't knowledge readily available except through prior experiences.

8

Learning Practical Wisdom

The best way to learn practical wisdom is through extensive experience in the work itself. Another way is to work on a project or as apprentice to a mentor who can convey by example what practical wisdom is all about. Yet another way to learn is vicariously through case studies of evaluations, such as the Denver project. Other than that, access to learning the practical wisdom of the craft is difficult. Evaluation experts can teach rules and methods, but the practical questions are if, when, and how to apply the rules and methods in actual situations. In other words, the practical is heavily contextual and circumstantial. Are there any other possibilities for learning practical wisdom?

For some time I've been concerned that the politics and ethics of evaluation in particular can't be captured very well by explicit analysis. That's because much of this knowledge is practical wisdom. Although excellent articles have outlined influences that affect evaluation politics in the abstract, novice evaluators still find themselves surprised by events they didn't foresee, motivations they didn't understand, and covert maneuvering they didn't expect.

Evaluating, pages 99–109

During a trip to England years ago, I was lamenting the difficulty of passing on such knowledge to younger people with my late colleague Barry MacDonald, one of the leading British evaluators (see Chapter 6). MacDonald was a veteran of many projects from which he gained practical knowledge through painful trial and error. After perhaps a dozen projects, evaluators eventually become seasoned. Is there a way for some of this knowledge to be passed on, short of listening to old timers tell stories?

Two events gave me a sense of direction. At the Center for Advanced Study in the Behavioral Sciences at Stanford in 2000, I gave a talk about the field of evaluation to the resident fellows there. The fellows were prominent social scientists unfamiliar with the practice of evaluation for the most part. They were intellectually a very smart group, but one without knowledge of either evaluation or the intricacies of education and social reforms. I condensed my talk into three themes meant to convey the progress of the evaluation field over the past several decades: causation, values, and politics.

When it came to formulating ideas about causation and values, I resorted to scholarly analysis by discussing the history of these concepts as they had developed in philosophy, social science, and evaluation, leading to certain controversies and their proper resolution. Although the Center fellows might disagree, they understood the issues. However, when it came to the politics of evaluation, I thought of few things to say, at least not much that would be enlightening to an audience short on evaluation experience. If I left out the politics, the fellows would have an inadequate understanding of what it means to conduct studies in settings where the politics can be intense. In many scholarly discussions, politics are bracketed out of consideration as being extraneous.

I couldn't reduce evaluation politics to scholarly categories to my satisfaction. What I did instead was tell a story about the evaluation of a complex program. The story illustrated several factors that evaluators encounter in conducting studies. This switch to a concrete story seemed to work well in conveying what I intended. Later that year, I gave a talk to the U.K. Evaluation Society, an audience consisting mostly of evaluators and government officials. They were well versed in the practice of evaluation. Again, stories about the politics of evaluation worked well.

Following these occasions, I began thinking about stories as a way to convey the politics and ethics of evaluation. One way was through a case study, such as I've presented about the Denver evaluation. Readers could experience events vicariously. Perhaps another way could be through a long story—maybe even a novel. The novel could be written with a view to inform, illustrate, and instruct. True, case studies are useful in conveying some dynamics of evaluations. However, a novel has some advantages. For one thing you can build into the novel what you want to illustrate. A novel can be constructed with deliberate lessons in mind. Second, the novel can be entertaining, something that makes the reader want to attend to the topic with enthusiasm. Case studies have a tendency to be a bit dull. Third, events in novels occur immediately as you read them, rather than being retrospective. You're presented with events as they occur. There is a sense of immediacy and engagement. Also, you can include events in a novel that you're not likely to include in a case study, including unsavory happenings likely to be omitted in case studies. Also, in fiction, you don't have to worry about libel suits. In other words, there are possibilities in fiction not available in case studies.

Over the next few years, I wrote an evaluation novel. When the manuscript was in reasonable shape, I showed a few colleagues, who were encouraging. Based on their suggestions, I revised the novel. When I was satisfied, I put it online to solicit broader comment. Some professors have used the novel to help them teach evaluation courses. Based on their comments, I revised the novel. The work is now in tested form, so to speak. (I'm an evaluator, after all.) It's this version of the work that I put into print (House, 2007).

Through the novel I was attempting to convey practical knowledge about evaluation, especially about the politics and ethics, along with everyday practical aspects of how evaluations work. I built several types of evaluation into the plot, including program evaluation, personnel evaluation, student evaluation, and meta-evaluation. I included different kinds of politics: the politician level, the department level, the bureaucratic level, and the personal level. I also built in several ethical issues and dilemmas. How ethical is it for evaluators to become romantically involved with clients? To seek revenge? To assist others in their ambitions? To ignore unethical conduct? To be loyal only to those who pay them?

These things happen in evaluations, and ordinarily the situations are not black and white. Always, there are extenuating circumstances. It's the complex, less clear-cut situations that tax our wisdom. I also tried to build into the novel how it feels to carry out evaluation tasks in planning and conducting evaluations, such as negotiating with clients, collecting information, analyzing data, writing reports, disseminating findings, and contending with negative client reactions and the media. In the novel, the main action occurs in a large city education bureaucracy that constitutes a world in itself, with its own rules, norms, and ambitions.

In short, the novel is meant to inform, enlighten, and entertain about the politics and ethics of evaluation. To make evaluation entertaining, a formidable challenge, I tried to generate interest by employing the mystery genre as the format, a genre well suited to evaluation, with the evaluator in the role of the investigating detective, yet doing recognizable evaluation tasks. Novels have to be entertaining, or else no one will read them. This novel is intended to provide a learning experience that combines love of mystery stories with insights into the nature of evaluation politics and ethics. By all accounts, the novel is readable. An additional appeal I discovered after I wrote the novel: readers become fascinated with trying to figure out what's true and what's fiction. Our old friend, the counterfactual, leads an active life in evaluation. By the way, the evaluation portrayed in the novel is not a deliberative democratic evaluation.

The novel is divided into seven parts, each with its own title—The Set Up, Consulting and Exploring, Reporting, Politics and Ethics, Disturbances, Publicity, and Revelation. With that said, let's look at a few scenes. We pick up the story as Paul Reeder, a university-based evaluator, has received a phone call from the New York City Mayor's office asking him to help oversee the evaluation of an important education program that's been the object of considerable public controversy. Reeder flies to New York to meet officials from the New York City school district for the first time.

FIRST ENCOUNTER (HOUSE, 2007, CHAPTER 3)

No matter how many times Reeder flew into New York, he was impressed with the skyline. The skyscrapers were not that much bigger than in Chicago or other cities. There were just so many of them. As the plane dipped slowly on its guide path in, he could see miles and miles of buildings, not just a cluster or two. Now, in the twilight, the buildings were lit up, which enhanced their mystery.

The school district contact had told him the administrators wanted to talk to him at the central offices in Brooklyn before he went to the Mayor's office the next morning. It was dark, nearly eight o'clock, before his taxi arrived at 110 Livingston Street. The building looked deserted. He checked through the security guard, who was expecting him, and took the elevator to the top floor, the Chancellor's offices.

The Deputy-Chancellor's office was dimly lit. He could see the lights of Manhattan skyscrapers in the background. Six men were waiting for him. A large African American man got up to shake his hand.

"Good to meet you. I'm Sam Kepner."

Kepner was Assistant Chancellor, the man Reeder had made arrangements with over the phone. Reeder had never met him but he knew his name. Kepner had spent years in Washington before coming to New York.

The man had a good reputation. He seemed affable enough.

The second man was the Deputy Chancellor, George Clough. He was tall, thin, stiff. Not so friendly. Probably the hatchet man.

Two men were in charge of departments, and the other two assistants. As Reeder shook their hands, Kepner motioned him to a chair against the wall. The six men sat down in a semicircle facing him.

"How was your flight?"

"Ok. A little bumpy coming in."

"Did you have any trouble getting in from the airport?"

"No, just some traffic at this time of evening." He felt tense, considering how the men were arrayed in front of him.

"Tomorrow you are going to meet with people from the Mayor's office. What we want you to understand tonight is who is paying you."

Kepner paused for a few moments to let his comment sink in.

"Although the Mayor's office chose you for the job, the money to pay you is coming from the school district. We are your employer. You understand that?" The way he said it was a command as much as a question.

He paused again. It was difficult for Reeder to read the expressions of the six men in the dim light. He sensed they were not friendly.

"You understand that?"

Kepner was waiting for a response.

Reeder hesitated. Until now he thought he was working for the Mayor. Clearly, the district had a different idea of who was in charge. He wondered if the Mayor's office had the same understanding. He would have to sort this out. But not here, not now.

"Yes, I understand that."

Reeder knew the money was coming from the school district. But it was coming at the insistence of the Mayor. Of course, Kepner was saying something else. He was saying who was boss. What Reeder didn't say was that he did not agree that who paid the bills called the shots, as they seemed to think.

"How much will your budget be?" Clough, the Deputy-Chancellor, entered the discussion for the first time.

"It depends what your evaluation consists of," Reeder said. "I haven't seen the evaluation plan."

The small nervous man in the navy blazer spoke.

"Essentially, we are collecting test scores for the students involved in the program and analyzing those. That's the evaluation in a nutshell."

Reeder figured this must be the head of the evaluation department, Rick Cole. He hadn't been able to keep their names straight after the introductions.

"Just test scores? Nothing else?" Reeder said. "Isn't that a little risky? It's pretty difficult to get gains on standardized tests. Hard to do. You might be setting the program up for failure."

"We are getting good gains already. Impressive gains. Besides, that's all anyone in this city is interested in, the test scores. So that is what we are giving them."

"If I were designing the evaluation, I would collect other kinds of information to balance off the tests."

"As I said, test scores are what people in New York are interested in. It wouldn't make any difference what the other information was. And the program results have been impressive so far."

So this is a one-ring circus, Reeder thought. He had given them his best advice about collecting other information. If that was what they wanted to do, ok. Their attitude was typical. Sponsors of new programs always thought their programs would raise test scores. Maybe they had to think that way to have the guts to try something new. But test scores were difficult to increase—unless you taught the test to the students. You could do it that way.

"You're doing all the data collection and analysis?"

"Right. The district—my office—collects the test data, and we analyze the scores. Then we publish reports on the program based on the results. The reports are public information."

The man was staking out his territory. To Reeder, maybe to the others. Probably a good move on his part.

"If we have access to the data and don't have to collect information ourselves, we can audit the evaluation for about seventy thousand dollars a year." Reeder dropped a number he had thought about on the plane.

"Jesus, that's a lot of money for simply looking over our shoulder!"

Kepner came back to life at the mention of money.

"Well, we need to make trips out here to check things out, maybe redo some of the data analyses. That budget would include our travel."

Reeder thought the budget was on the light side but figured he could get more from the district if needed, given the circumstances. If he lasted that long. It was difficult to estimate costs when you were unclear what the tasks were. Auditing someone else's evaluation was not the way things were done ordinarily.

"I can send you a budget when I get back. It could cost less."

There was no sense making this project a university contract. The university would take months to process the proposal and add a huge overhead to the budget costs. It was not set up to handle projects like this.

Kepner looked at Clough, the Deputy. No discernible sign passed between them, but Kepner said, "Ok, we can do that. We do need a detailed budget of estimated costs. We hold the money. You submit your claims to us for work completed."

"Well, as detailed as I can make it. I am guessing at what we are going to do."

"One page will be enough."

Three men had not said anything. Reeder guessed that the three doing the talking were the ones he had to deal with. And the Chancellor, wherever he was. No sign of him.

It was getting late. The men had spent a long day and were squirming in their chairs. Kepner suggested they quit and that Reeder take a taxi to his hotel in Manhattan. This neighborhood was no place to walk around this time of night. Reeder flagged a taxi at the door of the building while the security guard watched.

Manhattan was spectacular in the evening as the taxi arched across Brooklyn Bridge through traffic. The school district office was at one foot of the bridge and the Mayor's office at the other. As he crossed over the massive structure, Reeder remembered Hart Crane's poem about the bridge.

"How many dawns, chill from his rippling rest
The seagull's wings shall dip and pivot him,
Shedding white rings of tumult, building high
Over the chained bay waters Liberty—"

By chance, Crane wrote the poem in the same room from which the paralyzed engineer who built the bridge supervised its construction. Funny how things worked out. They reached the other side of the East River and entered Manhattan.

Commentary

What can we learn from this scene? First, we're in real time. This event is happening now, not in the past. As Reeder flies into New York, he can't help from being impressed by the majesty of the city and the setting he is entering. Both the setting and the unusual hour of the meeting are intimidating. The building is empty, another threatening sign. When he enters the office, he meets not one person, but half a dozen, intimidating once again. They array themselves around him, encircling him somewhat. This is a situation intended to impress and intimidate. Indeed, the situation is somewhat "noirish."

Not only is the setting shadowy, the circumstances surrounding the evaluation are as well. Who's really in charge? The Deputy Mayor's office contacted him originally, but these officials from the Chancellor's office are telling him they're in charge. The authority structure is ambiguous. The things Reeder doesn't know are considerably greater than the things he does know. Although the situation is dramatic and pitched at a grand scale to enhance the reader's interest, at the beginnning of most evaluations, evaluators often don't know very much. They're not sure who's really in charge. They have to make certain assumptions as to what's happening. It's only as the project progresses that they begin to understand. This is typical, though more dramatic and with larger consequences here.

One of the first things Reeder tries to do is figure out who's who and what the power structure is. He needs to know this to anticipate what may impede or disrupt the evaluation. In most cases, experienced evaluators do this intuitively as they go along. Here Reeder is immediately alert to who does the talking in this group. To whom must he attend? He soon picks out two key players by their actions in taking charge. Reeder wonders, among the key players, who wants what from the evaluation and from the education program? Reeder doesn't have to deliver what they want, and maybe he won't want to, but he needs to anticipate what the power players might do in pursuit of their goals. If this sounds complicated, humans have considerable capacity to figure out what other people want and what their intentions are. That's what it means to be social beings.

What does Reeder know at this moment? He knows this is a complicated operation that involves the power structure of the entire city. The call came from the Mayor's office. Now the men from the Chancellor's office say they're in charge. Reeder already knows that the project is important to the Mayor's reelection campaign and that the Deputy Mayor's office thinks the project will not succeed. From other sources Reeder has learned that the Comptroller's office, a separate entity, is extremely powerful in the city government. The Comptroller and the Mayor don't particularly like each other and, in fact, are competitors in running the city. In the complex power structure of city government, there are at least three powerful offices contending with each other. Each probably has different goals in mind for the project.

Reeder also knows at this stage that the evaluation is important. Otherwise, he would not have gotten a call from the Mayor's office inviting him to take on the project, and these six high ranking officials from the Chancellor's office would not have set this meeting up to orient and impress him with their point of view. If the evaluation were not important, they wouldn't have bothered. At this meeting, they are checking him out to see what type person they have to deal with. How seriously must they take him? How big a threat is he?

Reeder might seem far outmatched by those he's dealing with. But he has several things on his side. First, he is not from New York, which means they have limited means of threatening him at his own power base in the academic and evaluation world. His standing in his professional community is high. Furthermore, he has engaged in highly politicized evaluations before, and he knows how things work, though there is never an end to surprises. He's not surprised by this initial attempt to intimidate him. Furthermore, his character is such that intense conflicts are interesting. He enjoys political evaluations. They're a challenge.

Right now, Reeder is playing it cagey. When one of the men says, "We're paying you, do you understand that?" Reeder says, yes, he understands that. However, it's clear that the implication of the assertion is that Reeder is supposed to regard them as in charge since they are paying him. Reeder doesn't challenge the man's statement. He knows what the man means. However, in Reeder's mind, those who pay don't necessarily control the evaluation. As a matter of principle, an old colleague of his says, "Evaluations can be sponsored, but not purchased."

As Reeder heads across Brooklyn Bridge in a taxi, he recites lines from Hart Crane's poem about the bridge. The unusual sentence structure and grammar of Crane's poem presages troubles and "tumult" ahead. Reeder is anticipating challenges yet to come. The dark scene sets the mood and raises a question: Can evaluations be done properly in such intense political conditions? Perhaps it's the destiny of evaluators to create tumult and trouble.

Ideas for Teaching the Novel

Other than reading the novel to obtain some ideas, how might it be used for teaching purposes? Following are the ideas of three excellent teachers who have used the novel in teaching their evaluation courses.

Sharon Rallis

"Teaching With Novels: How I Use *Regression to the Mean*," Sharon Rallis, Dwight W. Allen Distinguished Professor, University of Massachusetts, Amherst.

I first used novels in my classroom when I taught high school history; I have never found any better way to bring alive events, concepts, people conflicts, and challenges—and to promote critical thinking. Now I teach about evaluation theory and practice to graduate students, so I am glad to have Ernie House's *Regression to the Mean: A Novel of Evaluation Politics* as a tool to bring evaluation alive. Following Paul Reeder as he interacts with all the different players in the evaluation of the *Second Chance* program, my students and I examine the challenges he faces and question his decisions and actions.

I divide my course into sections focusing on central questions: What is program evaluation: Purposes? Audiences? Approaches? What do we know about the program to be evaluated: Theory of action? Policy context? Stakeholder interests? Who is the evaluator: Perspective? Role? What decisions does or can the evaluator make for evaluation design and then while implementing?

I assign the novel at the beginning of the semester, asking for a few chapters a week. Once they begin, many students read through quickly because it is, after all, a novel. Each week at the end of class we ask questions about Reeder's actions and his situation, analyzing and critiquing aspects that are relevant to the week's topic. For example, when discussing program theory, we consider on what theory *Second Chance* was grounded—and whether all players agreed. We discuss how Reeder figured it out—and what difference any theory made for the evaluation. We "ask" Reeder several questions: How does he discover the program theory? How does he judge its implementation? What are his data sources—and what does he count as credible evidence?

In another class we look closely at Reeder as the evaluator. We "ask" him: Why is he qualified to conduct *this* evaluation? Might reasons exist why he should not evaluate this program? How does he decide how to interact with various stakeholders? What is his approach or perspective? What role or roles does he take—and why? How do they change?

Reeder and *Second Chance* are especially useful when we study decisions regarding evaluation design and implementation. We usually spend considerable time examining what I call the everyday choices evaluators make as theory hits practice, that is, when conducting the actual evaluation: Which decisions (Reeder's or other influential players) seem to be critical? On what grounds were the decisions made? Who benefited? Who was harmed? When does Reeder have control (or not) over his choices or actions? When might players have treated others differently (e.g., more respectfully)? When did a decision or action result in injustices? Why? What could Reeder have been done differently? Often the class ends with students proposing alternative scenarios.

Each semester the questions and dialogue differ, depending on how students interpret the novel and how they choose to apply what they are learning about evaluation to their interpretations. Often we simulate question and answers with Reeder; other times we critique. Always, reading and talking about Reeder in the novel generates provocative and enlightening class conversation.

Katherine Ryan

Professor Katherine Ryan, University of Illinois, has used the novel to teach an advanced educational evaluation course by linking chapters to abstract substantive material. She prepares a small vignette play based on the novel to be acted out in class. Students pretend to be the "team" that Reeder puts together to do the New York project, and they answer questions like these as a group activity:

a. You are engaging in an evaluation service (meta-evaluation, audit, evaluation). Which one? How do you define it? Do a cursory analysis using dimensions of educational accountability. What is the theory of action in New York or the theory of teaching and learning? How is the New York City case different from NCLB requirements?

b. Based on your analysis, what issues do you see? What's your plan for implementing the evaluation service? We've discussed different evaluation approaches in class (evaluation research, responsive evaluation, evaluation as educational accountability, evaluation as social inquiry, evaluation as social criticism.) What are the theoretical roots of your plan?

c. How would you describe the internal evaluation approach that's being used to evaluate "Second Chance" in the novel?

Professor Ryan also uses the novel as an introduction to evaluation methods by tying various chapters to substantive material, such as context, ethics, fielding the evaluation request, and negotiating the evaluation. These concepts are difficult for students to understand, and the novel provides illustrations.

___

Kevin Welner

Professor Kevin Welner, University of Colorado Boulder, has used the novel as a primary text that introduces the students to the field of evaluation with action, colorful characters, and controversial issues, or as a supplementary text linked to other readings. For example, he's used the novel in the first or second week of class as an illustration that's returned to throughout the semester. Alternatively, he's used it near the end of class as a reflective and culminating story. In the first use, the novel provides a shared evaluation experience that becomes part of the class's common language. When he introduces or explores an evaluation model, he uses the novel's story as factual backdrop (e.g., "What if Reeder had used this approach?)" In the second use, the novel offers a backdrop against which to project the models and ideas introduced during the class. Of course, how the novel is used in teaching a course is up to each instructor. There is no one best way to use it.

9

When to Rely on Practical Wisdom

When does someone possess practical wisdom that is valid? In professional fields, practical wisdom is close to what we call clinical expertise. Research findings about the validity of clinical expertise in different fields are mixed. However, the explanation for these mixed results provides support for the validity of practical wisdom and clinical expertise *under the right conditions*. In this chapter, I'll consider the question of when practical wisdom is valid and discuss a few more examples of practical wisdom in evaluation. The short answer is that validity depends on the field one is engaged in, the type of task being performed, and how much experience the expert has. The confidence of the practitioner is not a good indicator of validity since practitioners tend to be over confident about what they are doing.

In *Thinking Fast and Slow,* Kahneman (2011) reports that he has long been skeptical about the validity of clinical expertise. On the one hand, there is the research about psychologists predicting student grades in college, political experts forecasting political events, and stock experts picking high performing stocks (Meehl, 1954). Typically, these predictions have low validity, achieving results no better than simple algorithms can do (See

Evaluating, pages 111–126
111

Kahneman, Chapters 20, 21, 22). On the other hand, the research on decisions made by experienced firefighters, clinical nurses, and physicians demonstrate high validity. Why is there such a difference?

Firefighters can draw on the repertoire of patterns they've experienced over decades of service. They can simulate a pattern mentally to see if it would work in this particular situation and modify it, if necessary. In Kahneman's terms, the process involves both Systems 1 and 2 thinking. After stimulation by some clue, System 1 produces a plan based on the patterns stored in the associative memory. This is pattern recognition. System 2 checks out the plan. In these validity studies, the firefighters and nurses were not required to make long-term forecasts beyond the range of their immediate experiences. This is a significant factor since their knowledge is based on what they have observed.

Where does the pattern come from? It comes from experience. For complex tasks, expertise takes a long time to develop. Expertise is not a single skill but a collection of many skills. For example, studies of chess masters have shown that high performance takes about 6 years of playing chess 5 hours a day. During hours of intense concentration, chess players become familiar with thousands of configurations. Like chess players, successful clinicians practice in environments that are quite regular, if complex. Physicians, nurses, athletes, and firefighters also face regular situations. Stock pickers and political scientists operate in low validity environments where there are many factors they don't know about that can invalidate long-term forecasts. Both the specific tasks the experts perform and the area in which the experts are engaged make a significant difference in the validity of the expertise.

The two conditions necessary for acquiring valid expertise are, first, an environment that's regular enough to be predictable, and, second, an opportunity to learn these regularities through long practice. By contrast, clinical psychologists in validity studies were assigned tasks that did not have a simple solution. After all, clinicians don't usually have a chance to see what happens to students and patients years later. In the validity studies, they were asked to forecast in an unpredictable world, an impossible task for anyone. Intuitions can't be trusted without regularities in the environments in which the practitioners work. Professionals need a chance to develop expertise that depends on the quality and speed of feedback and on an opportunity to practice, preferably with direct feedback on their performance. Therapists can be highly skilled in understanding a patient's mind, but still unable to predict long-term outcomes of treatments because accurate feedback on treatment outcomes is usually not available to them. There are too many intervening factors that influence the treatment outcomes.

In less regular environments, System 1 will invoke some heuristic to provide an explanation, such as substituting a different question to answer. For example, in forecasting whether a company's stock is worth purchasing, stock pickers will often resort to judging the company executives. The quality of the executive is something one can ascertain, but it has low predictability for the stock's investment potential. For example, the current value of a stock is critical to its future performance, whatever the quality of the CEO. "If the environment is sufficiently regular and if the judge has had a chance to learn its regularities, the associative machinery will recognize situations and generate quick and accurate predictions and decisions. You can trust someone's intuitions if these conditions are met" (Kahneman, 2011, p. 242).

What about evaluators? The practical wisdom of evaluators fits the high validity situation, in my view, depending on what we are talking about. Most of the situations evaluators face have considerable regularity. In fact, I would be surprised if experienced evaluators do not recognize many of the evaluation situations I have been presenting. Second, highly experienced evaluators have an opportunity to learn these regularities over time and to recognize patterns. In other words, they are able to acquire practical wisdom in pursuing their craft. However, this conclusion applies only to work with which the evaluators have immediate contact, which is what we are discussing here. For example, I would not expect evaluators to be able to predict exactly what effects the findings of their evaluations would have within large, complex organizations. They would not have much experience with the internal workings of the organizations that absorb these findings, and these organizations would be quite diverse. Again, there are too many intervening influences on what happens. One important conclusion is that evaluators should recognize the boundaries within which their practical wisdom resides. I've already discussed both the danger of overconfidence and the utility of including an "outside view" to mitigate overconfidence (Chapter 5).

The Evaluation Report as Political Document

In the evaluation novel introduced in the last chapter, Paul Reeder, the evaluator, has established an evaluation team to conduct a review of the New York City Second Chance program. His team found that the evaluation of the summer training program has produced some erroneous findings. In their analysis, the district evaluators have failed to account for regression to the mean. Although the district claims there are substantial test score gains from their summer training program, the training program has produced no gains at all after adjusting for the regression effects. Furthermore, the Mayor has used the summer findings in his reelection campaign as evidence that his education plan for the city is working. How does Reeder handle writing a report that says there are no gains, a potentially explosive finding?

CHAPTER 21 (HOUSE, 2007)

Reeder rose early next morning and was in the office by seven. He needed a clear head and no interruptions to write the New York report. He figured it should be short, no more than ten pages. People in the Mayor and Chancellor's offices didn't have time to read long documents.

The blend of the technical and non-technical was tricky. He had technical readers in the evaluation personnel but non-technical ones in the political offices. And he had a difficult topic, the mistaken test score gains due to regression. He would have to strike a balance in making the report readable for the non-technical readers while making it authoritative for those who could understand the test score analysis.

How positive and how negative should he be? The message was that the test score gains were non-existent. That message alone was too negative. He could balance that conclusion with an assessment of the evaluation plan the district had developed, which was not bad, and throw in a reference to Mrs. Douglas's class to provide hope that things might improve.

This tact might prove to be too positive if no gains in test scores developed, but no one knew at this time. Simply because there were no gains during the summer didn't mean there would be none during the academic year when students had more time in Second Chance classes.

Reeder thought about his report as he drove to the office. Once he had a cup of coffee in hand, he fired up his computer. He jotted down five topics he wanted to cover—an introduction that set the tone, a review of the plan, a challenge to the test gains, a look at Mrs. Douglas's classroom, and suggestions to strengthen the evaluation design. He took a sip of coffee and plunged ahead. He wrote quickly, knowing he could backtrack. The first task was to get the ideas down.

He worked steadily for two hours, pausing to think for a few minutes at a time, then jotting down more ideas. It was easy until he got to the regression. He thought of ways to convey the concept that would be meaningful for those who didn't understand tests. When he bogged down, he got up from his desk and poured another coffee from the pot in the seminar room. He was getting himself wired with caffeine.

In two hours he had seven pages. Now for revision. He went back to the beginning to read the report through for flow and clarity. He rewrote sentences, replaced words, and moved phrases to the front or back of sentences to make references clear. He noticed spots where he jumped from one thought to another abruptly. He added connections between sections.

An interesting thing about writing was that he never knew exactly what he was going to say until he wrote it. He worked from a brief outline, a few phrases placed at the beginning of the document, at least with a paper this short. Usually he was surprised by what he had said when he was done.

For this report he invented examples to explain the regression effect. To improve the evaluation design, he suggested doing case studies, like Mrs. Douglas's class, in which others could see the program functioning. By the time he finished, he had eight pages.

He read back through the document looking at each word carefully. He knew from sorrowful experience that readers could bounce off the wall by catching the nuance of a single wrong word. Words that attributed bad motives to people were explosive. People felt their worth was being examined, and they could hardly take comments impersonally. Usually he could catch trip words before he sent the report. Sometimes he couldn't and found them only from negative reactions. He wanted readers to focus on the ideas he wanted to convey, not on misunderstandings.

As he finished, Reeder was pleased with the way it looked. There were two points he wasn't sure about. He wasn't sure if he had compromised the regression explanation too much, and he wasn't sure what to say about minorities. He would discuss these with his team. If you were working with a team, it was a good idea to allow them to make contributions.

By the time he finished and leaned back in his chair, it was nearly eleven. He had been lucky that he had no interruptions. A good morning's work. Maybe the New York project would go smoothly after all. He sent an email to his colleagues to arrange a meeting, attaching an electronic copy of the draft to the message. Time for a swim.

Commentary

Reeder faces a difficult task in writing this report. The message is negative because the test score gains from the summer program are non-existent. The district evaluators have neglected to account for regression to the mean, a difficult concept to understand. He tries to soften the blow of the negative message while offering some way for the audience to understand the technical aspects. Why not just give them the bad news and let it go at that?

Evaluation audiences are human, like evaluators. In this case, the district personnel have come to believe that the summer program was a smashing success. It will take quite some time for them to come to grips with the bad news. Evaluators seriously underestimate how long it takes for people to assimilate bad news. It takes a considerable amount of time to move the mental furniture around. Changing minds requires not just changing one fact, but changing the entire network of ideas related to it. If the summer program didn't work, many other ideas must be readjusted. This takes a lot of mental work over a period of time, and usually there is considerable emotion mixed in with the changes.

By offering them some positive news and some hope that things might get better, Reeder makes the bad news more palatable. Of course, he doesn't want to overdo the optimism. He's finding something positive and genuine to balance the bad news. His purpose long term is to improve the overall evaluation of the program. If he is entirely negative at the beginning, they are likely to reject his assessment altogether. He has his mind focused on the ultimate effects of his engagement with them. And although the summer program has not produced dramatic results, as they had mistakenly concluded, that is no reason to declare the entire academic year program a failure either.

As for explaining regression to the mean, he might not try to explain it. If he does try, he might say something like this. Imagine selecting the lowest twenty percent of students on a reading test. Some might have scored so low because of poor reading ability. Others may have done even more poorly because they also had the flu, stayed up late watching television, or were emotionally upset because their parents had gotten into a fight. If you give the same test again, these unlucky students, back to normal, will score higher. Of course, other students will score lower because similar things happened to them in the meantime.

But, wait a minute. Many of the students who had scored lower the second time around are not in the already selected bottom twenty percent group because they were placed in the top eighty percent in the initial selection process. They're not in the program at all. You can't count their lower scores in the group. The outcome of this extreme selection procedure is that the lower twenty percent group will improve on the test scores the second time around. In other words, the overall scores will regress toward the mean. There is a way of correcting for the regression effect, but sometimes the gains attributable to regression are mistaken for real test score gains.

Regression to the mean is a very difficult concept to understand. It was first identified and explained by Galton, with considerable effort and help from the leading statisticians of his day, two hundred years after the discovery of gravity (Kahneman, 2011, Chapter 17). Whether the evaluator would attempt even a partial explanation, such as I've given, would depend on the audience and circumstances of the evaluation. Ordinarily, I would say not to attempt it, but it depends on the particular audience for the report.

Challenges to Findings

Reeder has sent the report to the Chancellor and Mayor's offices. He has heard nothing for two weeks. Ominous. Suddenly, he has a call to come meet the Chancellor. The Chancellor is angry and wants to talk to Reeder face to face. Reeder travels to New York City and waits two days in a hotel room for a call. Nothing. Suddenly, he receives a message to meet the Vice-Chancellor at the school district offices.

CHAPTER 28 (HOUSE, 2007)

Next morning, his third day in town, the telephone in his hotel room rang. He was recovering from the night before. He had not gotten back to the hotel until early morning. It was Kepner, calling to tell him to come to the district administration building.

"We want you to come over to the Chancellor's office at ten. The Chancellor has an emergency and is too busy to see you, but George Clough, the Deputy, will see you. You met him before."

The hatchet man, Reeder thought. And from his appearance, an effective one. Reeder recalled the shadowy meeting during his first trip to town.

"Will you be there?" he asked.

"No, just you and the Deputy. The two of you."

That made it easier for the Deputy to deny what was said between them, if that became necessary. Reeder had no colleague with him. He had to play the cards he had been dealt.

"Ok, ten o'clock. His office?"

"Yes." Kepner seemed less friendly. Something in his voice that wasn't there before. He gave no clue about the agenda. Reeder didn't ask. They had decided what to do with him.

It was a brisk, sunny day, though still cold. The traffic through town and onto the bridge was heavy. They drove over Brooklyn Bridge slowly, and Reeder thought about Velma working in her office nearby. He arrived at 110 Livingston Street ten minutes early. He took the elevator to the top floor, pulling his flight bag behind him. The Deputy's secretary greeted him and seated him across from her desk. She didn't seem friendly either. Funny how assistants picked up vibes from their bosses.

The door to the Deputy's office was open, and Reeder could see in. The Deputy was sitting on a couch watching television. No one was in the office with him. Ten o'clock came and Reeder waited. Ten fifteen.

The Deputy disappeared from view, presumably to go to his desk, which Reeder couldn't see from his chair. Finally, at ten-thirty Deputy Clough rang the secretary to admit Reeder.

"You can go in now." She shut the door behind him.

The space was large, a corner office looking out over the city. It would make ten of Reeder's cubicle at the university. The Deputy was seated at an imposing oak desk facing the door. An American flag was on one side behind him and a New York flag on the other. Two couches formed an "L" near the television, which was turned off now. The furniture looked as if it had been around for a while, including the television set.

The Deputy rose from behind the desk, shook his hand without saying a word, and motioned Reeder to sit at the couch. He was half a head taller and leaner. He unbuttoned his coat. He didn't speak until he sat down on the other couch.

"I thought we hired you guys to help us, not hurt us." The Deputy was not smiling as he looked at Reeder.

"Well, we are trying to help you." It sounded feeble.

"Your report says that we don't have any test gains from the program. That doesn't help us. It makes us look bad." The report was not in sight anywhere. Clough knew what he wanted to say about it.

"True, but it saves you the embarrassment of someone from the outside finding out your testing office has not used the correct statistical analysis." Reeder cleared his throat.

"Look," the Deputy said, "You professors are a dime a dozen. I can hire professors to say anything I want them to say. Anytime I want. Right here in this city."

Reeder knew Clough was right. He could hire someone to say what he wanted. He was resorting to outright intimidation. Nothing disguised about it.

"Maybe so. But this regression analysis is not arbitrary. There's a right way and a wrong way to do it. You might hire someone to say what you want but sooner or later, someone outside New York, if not someone inside, will discover that the district has done the analysis wrong. And blow the whistle. Second Chance is a nationally known program. You'll be embarrassed. Better to face up to it and fix it now rather than later."

"That's your opinion. There are other experts around. And more than one way to do statistical analysis."

"Look, pretend that I'm a weapons expert, and I tell you that the bullets you are using in your gun are not the right caliber. And that sooner or later the gun is going to blow up in your hand if you continue to use that ammunition. I've have given you my best professional advice. If you want to take your chances anyhow, then go ahead. Fire away."

Reeder sat back on the couch, finished. The Deputy was silent for more than a full minute, which seemed to Reeder a long, long time. Neither man said anything, while Clough thought it over. Reeder had formulated the analogy, anticipating a negative reception. He thought the gun analogy was particularly appropriate for New York. He could hear horns honking and traffic on the streets below.

Finally, the Deputy said, "Well, ok. What if we do this? We put our analysis of the test scores into our report. Our analysis shows the gains. Then we add another page that shows the analysis based on the regression analysis. Your analysis, which shows no gains, on the next page. Readers would have both. Would that satisfy you?" His voice was softer, conciliatory.

"I think we can live with that," Reeder said right away, relieved the impasse had been broken. The tension between them drained away.

They spent fifteen minutes talking about details of Reeder's report. Reeder left the office wondering if Clough would turn the television back on. The confrontation had been over quicker than Reeder expected, though it had been intense. Head on. Sometimes encounters like these lasted days or weeks. He picked up his bag in the outer office, thanked the secretary, who said nothing, and caught a taxi to LaGuardia.

Commentary

Reeder has come through a harrowing experience of having to present bad news face to face with the sponsor of the work. The evaluation analysis is challenged point blank, and Reeder's own authority is questioned. From the beginning, the VC's plan is to intimidate Reeder. They make Reeder wait for two days before the meeting with no explanation. When Reeder arrives on time, the VC makes him wait for half an hour while letting Reeder see him watching television, an appearance of unconcern and Reeder's unimportance. The VC's office is huge and impressive.

The initimidation pattern is a continuation of the first meeting and, obviously, a favorite way that the district administrators deal with others. The VC reminds Reeder that they have hired him to help them, a reference back to the first meeting when they reminded him he was working for them. Why is it that Reeder is now trying to hurt them, an implicit plea of injury and betrayal? Without renouncing the pay for play relationship directly, Reeder plays along. He is trying to help them, he says. He doesn't want them to be embarrassed. The VC plays his trump card: professors are a dime a dozen, and he can hire them to say whatever he wants. Reeder has been around enough to realize there is considerable truth to this. Academics are particularly influenced and intimidated by powerful administrators, whether in big cities, state capitals, or Washington. Many academics are afraid to criticize authority.

No doubt this is a prime reason the Deputy Mayor's office decided to hire a meta-evaluator from some distance away, someone with a tough reputation. They knew the meta-evaluator would be up against tough opposition. Reeder has a couple of things on his side. He's from outside NYC, and there's not much they can do to him personally. Furthermore, he's sure of his evaluation analysis. He has a leading authority on his team. Reeder plays his own trump card. The VC may dismiss the analysis, but sooner or later, it will blow up in his face. Reeder relies on his own power base, academic authority. Reeder's confidence and unwillingness to back down impresses the VC, who suggests a compromise. They will include both analyses in the report that the district makes public. This isn't a perfect solution, but Reeder figures it's good enough. It gives the district a face-saving way out without forcing the district to take a die-hard stand against the report. It leaves the door open for future cooperation towards improving the Second Chance evaluation. Sometimes evaluators are wise to be practical, rather than perfect. When it comes to practical wisdom, evaluation ethics and politics are high on the priority list.

Note

For those interested in the evaluation novel, see House (2007). The attached appendix provides a discussion guide to the novel. Also, see suggestions for teaching the novel in the previous chapter, Chapter 8.

Appendix: Discussion Questions
for *Regression to the Mean* (House, 2007)

Part 1: The Setup

1. From the beginning of the novel, it's obvious that the evaluation is going to be used politically in the interaction between the Mayor and the Chancellor's offices. Some stakeholders see the evaluation as arbiter, some as bargaining tool, and some as leverage. What stakeholder groups are involved? Should Reeder have taken on the project under these circumstances? What safeguards are at his disposal?

2. On his first trip to New York to negotiate the project, Reeder is pressured by the Chancellor's men. ("Remember who you are working for.") Should he attend to those who pay him and ignore the other stakeholders? What should he include in his agreement with these clients? By the time he arrives, much of the evaluation design is already determined. Other than test scores, what else might the evaluation of have included? In what other ways might Reeder's own monitoring be conducted?

3. In his evaluation of police training in a U.S. southern state, what mistakes has Andrew Neil made? In what ways has he over-estimated his capacity to manage the situation? Is a situation ever too politicized for an evaluator to take on? What are some of Neil's strong and weak qualities as an evaluator, based on this brief glimpse of him?

4. Neil advises Reeder to build a team to help him in the New York project. What qualities is Reeder looking for in his team? What qualities has he omitted that he might have considered? Is his concern about minority politics justified, or is this merely "political correctness" on his part?

5. The department faculty meeting provides a few laughs. What's the role of evaluation in this faculty meeting? In making fun of the self-importance of faculty members, is the author merely poking fun at university faculty or is there some truth to this characterization?

Part 2: Consulting and Exploring

6. The physical description of the city of Washington announces it as a place of power politics. What is the general power hierarchy, as implied by the novel? Who are the major players? How does evaluation fit into this hierarchy?

7. At the National Science Foundation, Reeder assumes the role of a consultant. How would you describe his role and attitude? How does this differ from his role as evaluator?

8. In the proposed evaluation of science, math, and engineering education programs across the federal government, Reeder suggests a "blue ribbon" panel evaluation. Why is it appropriate for this occasion? What are the strengths and weaknesses of such an approach?

9. In his second trip to New York, Reeder visits Rick Cole, the director of evaluation in the city schools, to determine whether Cole and his colleagues are deliberately ignoring the regression effect, thereby inflating test score gains. What difference might such deception make to Reeder, if deliberate? What difference might it make for the Second Chance evaluation and the monitoring?

10. Reeder visits a New York school without clear prior expectations in his mind as to what he might find there. Why might exploring the unknown in a project be a good idea for an evaluator? What does he find? What difference could this make for his monitoring?

11. So far, we have a glimpse of the New York and Washington politics influencing evaluations. How are these politics similar? How different? How could the politics affect the evaluations?

Part 3: Reporting

12. Reeder has come to the point of writing his first report to his New York clients. What considerations does he have in mind as he prepares the report? Do these seem reasonable? What else might he have thought about? What advice does he solicit from his colleagues on the evaluation team? What seem to be his rules for handling his team?

13. His first report is not well received since it contains bad news. Although the pressures exerted by the New Yorkers are unusually confrontational, evaluators do come under fire for negative findings. Did Reeder handle himself appropriately? What else might he have done? How do you think you would behave in the face of such negative feedback? How might you prepare for negative reactions?

14. Meanwhile, Reeder has started a love affair with Velma, one of his clients. Is this a smart thing to do? Is it ethical? What might be some negative consequences of such a relationship?

15. Back at the university the campus promotions committee is evaluating colleagues for promotion. What faculty norms and rules seem to govern such behavior? The committee has encountered an unusual problem with an archeology professor. How do you

think they should handle it? How do the norms shape what is possible in the evaluation?

16. Finally, Reeder comes face to face with a student he is grading and frankly doesn't like. How do the rules for evaluating students differ from those for evaluating colleagues? Are students truly subject to unfair evaluations like this, or is Reeder's behavior unusual? How could evaluation of students be handled better?

Part 4: Politics and Ethics

17. In the case of the promotion of the archeology professor at the university, why is the committee still having such a difficult time deciding what to do? How else might they proceed, knowing what they know now?

18. Was the omission of the last page of the New York evaluation report an oversight or deliberate, in your opinion? Reeder wonders what to do about the missing page, and Andrew Neil advises him not to mention it. That will give Reeder an advantage in dealing with the school district. (They will know that he knows, but he doesn't mention it. So they may think he always knows more than he says, which gives him an advantage.) Is this a good way of handling the problem? Is it ethical?

19. When Reeder suspects some schools might be cheating on the tests, how does he check out this possibility? What else might he have done to confirm his suspicions? Should he have ignored the cheating and kept to his appointed tasks?

20. When he is convinced enough to present his suspicions to the school district, Rick Cole already knows about the cheating, though he has said nothing. Indeed, Cole places the responsibility on Reeder's shoulders. How typical of bureaucratic behavior do you think this is? Should Cole have been more forthcoming?

21. So far, Reeder has encountered several situations where ethical problems might be involved? What are some examples? How typical are such situations in evaluation studies in your view?

Part 5: Disturbances

22. In the promotions of the business professor who helped the governor and the art professor who made artwork from rugs, the promotion committee has run into difficulties again. Viewed as evaluations, what problems do these cases present to the evaluating committee?

23. The field of evaluation has developed a small industry that specializes in conducting evaluations by contract. What problems might "contracting out" evaluations present for officials? What problems might the evaluations present for contractors? What ethical problems might arise?

24. In his talk to the NSF board, Reeder briefly traces the history of the evaluation field. In fielding questions he says evaluation is not a science. Do you agree? Is evaluation a discipline? A profession? Reeder also points out the difficulties of evaluating research studies in particular. What are some of these difficulties?

25. Why are people tempted to cheat on the tests in the NY schools? How common a problem is this in schools? How might the Chancellor's drive and charisma exacerbate the problem? What are some ways of easing the conflict between those who believe in their programs and those who must evaluate them?

26. When Reeder meets parents of failed students, he becomes disconcerted listening to their testimony about the effects of failing. Yet he can do nothing about it within the terms of his prescribed role, in his own view. Do you think he is correct about this limitation of his role? Was it wise of him to accept the project on these conditions? Although there is substantial research about the effects of retaining students, previous research seems to have played little part in the Second Chance program or its evaluation. In general, what part should previous research play in evaluations, if any?

Part 6: Publicity

27. When Andrew Neil speaks to the evaluation class, he suggests deliberately inserting false data into evaluation reports to empower audiences by lessening the authority of evaluators. This is extreme, to say the least. What are some better ways of encouraging dialogue about findings? Is encouraging dialogue necessary or desirable?

28. Reeder is cast into the public limelight by the *Village Voice* exposé of the Second Chance program. How well does he handle the spotlight? How else might he have responded to media attention?

29. His testimony to the City Council has pitfalls as well as advantages. What are the advantages of speaking directly to members of the public like this? What are some disadvantages? How might the evaluator prepare for such encounters?

30. Tom Kepler's disclosure that Chancellor Pellegrini is borrowing money from his subordinates puts Reeder in an awkward position.

What should Reeder do about it? What can he do? Is his reasoning sound?

31 Apparently, Reeder has put his professional evaluation skills to good use in financial investing. What evaluation skills might carry over to investing? What prevents these skills from being applied to his relationship with Velma? How appropriate is it to employ such skills in such a relationship?

Part 7: Revelations

32. Neil reminds Reeder that revenge is not an appropriate motive for evaluators. Do you agree? What might Reeder have done to work through his emotions?

33. What might Reeder have done to manage his emotions towards Velma better? Has he been fair to her? Should he have been in this situation to begin with?

34. Should Reeder have informed the press about Chancellor Pellegrini's scheme? How should he have handled this information? How many options for the evaluator can you think of in such a situation?

35. In the end, was the monitoring of the New York evaluation a success? How do you think Reeder will feel about it later?

36. Neil quotes Freud: "The voice of the intellect is a soft one, but it does not rest until it has gained a hearing. Ultimately, after endless rebuffs, it succeeds. This is one of the few points on which one can be optimistic about the future of mankind." How does this quote apply to this particular evaluation? How does it apply to evaluation generally?

Overall

37. You've seen Reeder engaged in several evaluations in this novel. What are his strengths as an evaluator? His weaknesses? What advice would you give him to improve?

38. Recall three different evaluation situations from the book? How did the "authority structure" in each setting affect the evaluations? How did the politics?

39. This book and these questions have focused on the politics and ethics of evaluation, even on emotions, rather than on methods. Nonetheless, what methodological issues did you note? How did they interact with the politics and ethics? Might Reeder have avoided problems by using other methods?

40. Reeder sizes up the political situation and each person's presumed role in it when he enters a new situation. Why might this be important for the evaluation? How could you do it systematically?

41. At the beginning, Reeder is set back by the New York demand for confidential reports. What's wrong with confidential reports, as opposed to public reports? What circumstances might justify confidential reports? Who should have control over reports generally?

42. When he thinks clients are making wrong assumptions, Reeder informs them of his opinion without arguing with them. Is this a reasonable way to handle such disagreement? What is the ethical thing to do?

10

Conclusion

Twenty-Five Ideas

1. *Evaluating is a natural thought process that enables humans to assess their environment.* Evaluating is a primary strategy by which humans adjust to the world. Values emerge from our interactions with each other and with the world. They are integral components of our thinking processes.

2. *Core thinking is evaluative.* Our basic thought processes are evaluative. What cognitive researchers call fast and slow thinking are both evaluative. Fast thinking operates intuitively, engages most of the time, and detects deviations from normal. Slow thinking operates analytically, engaging when deviations occur and dealing with them.

3. *Values are real in the sense that they are natural, come from biological processes, and are a product of evolution.* There has been a long debate in philosophy and the social sciences as to the ontological status of values. The traditional view is that values are projections onto the world. However, from an evolutionary viewpoint, they are natural and enhance survival. Since we are part of nature, we engage in and with nature to determine what we value.

4. *Evaluators evaluate with their whole person, not only with methods.* There are many aspects of evaluating that methods of professional

Evaluating, pages 127–131
127

evaluation don't address, such as how rigorous the conclusions are and how we present findings. Thinking entails marked physiological changes. The more difficult the mental tasks, the more marked the changes, for example, blood pressure rises and the heart rate increases.

5. *Many personal values, traits, and dispositions, are derived from childhood, family, and community.* Mostly, these traits, dispositions, and values are advantageous, but not always. Early personal values and dispositions have a long reach.

6. *The personal values of evaluators strongly affect how they conduct studies.* As with other professionals, value differences among evaluators are acceptable within limits. Opportunism and ideological rigidity on the part of evaluators are beyond the acceptable limits.

7. *Humans are rational most of the time, but not perfectly and not always.* Contrary to the assumptions of classic economic theory, humans are not perfectly rational in calculating their interests all the time. They are rational much of the time, but often deviate because of biases in their thinking.

8. *Some thinking biases are attributable to the architecture of our cognitive machinery.* To arrive at reasonably accurate decisions quickly, humans have evolved thinking heuristics that sometimes produce systematic errors. These errors are similar from person to person and result from substituting speed and ease of thinking for more accuracy.

9. *Biases are a good way to understand evaluative thinking.* Key evaluation frameworks, like Campbell and Stanley's conception of experimental validity and Scriven's conception of objectivity, focus on potential biases. In cognitive research, Kahneman and Tversky's investigations into cognitive thinking processes focused on biases.

10. *Being objective means protecting against biases, broadly conceived, in addition to employing methods, more narrowly conceived.* The way to valid findings is to check carefully for biases that may produce errors and to correct for these. Although traditional methods correct for some biases, employing the same methods in every situation is inadequate because biases vary from one situation to another, and not all biases are connected to methods.

11. *Evaluators are immersed in the real world.* Evaluators participate in the world in the deepest sense. They are subject to the same biases, political pressures, and temptations as other people. They need to be aware of their embedded situation to protect them-

selves and their craft. This idea is in opposition to the belief that evaluators are immune to pressures because they are evaluators.

12. *Evaluator biases are common.* Evaluators can draw incorrect conclusions by being too sympathetic to the wrong people or by being ignorant of critical missing data. However, there are safeguards for dealing with these biases. The first safeguard is to be aware of the possibilities for bias.

13. *Basing evaluations on the views of diverse stakeholders addresses several biases to which evaluators are vulnerable.* Including a broad variety of stakeholder views and interests helps protect against the possibility of some biases. Considering only a few stakeholder views risks ignoring key outcomes and unanticipated side effects. In general, a diversity of views alerts the evaluator to possibilities.

14. *Professional evaluation is an institutional embodiment of evaluative thinking.* Since we have natural evaluating capabilities, we need not start anew as professional evaluators. We can organize the professional community to promote valid evaluations and the procedures by which we arrive at them. We can institutionalize our knowledge of what constitutes valid evaluating.

15. *Professional evaluation and the social sciences are value-imbued, not value-free.* In spite of long-standing confusion over the nature of values, professional evaluation and the social sciences are based on values. The fact/value dichotomy, a mistaken view of both facts and values, developed from Enlightenment thinking that separated the "self" from the natural world. Values were conceived as projected onto the world rather than being part of it. In fact, humans are in the world, and values emerge from interacting with it.

16. *The professional evaluation community has its own set of values.* The professional evaluation community has values that are central to the enterprise. These include rationality, consistency, logic, honesty, and reflectivity. For example, deliberate falsification of findings would be abhorred, an ethical value, as would lack of sufficient support for conclusions, an epistemic value.

17. *Evaluation is a communal process, as well as an individual process.* Several communal influences are at work in conducting evaluations. These include the values and understandings from the community in which the evaluation is taking place, the community from which the evaluator comes, and the evaluation community, of which the evaluator is a member. Culturally responsive evaluation is an example of such interaction. For a deeper analysis we should

examine the values and understandings of the evaluation community and the home community of the evaluator.

18. *Both factual claims and value claims can be objective if assessed rationally.* These claims can be objective in the sense that they can be argued, supported by evidence, and carefully assessed with the reasoning, data collections, analyses, and procedures that we recognize in the evaluation community as valid.

19. *Individual evaluators can improve the evaluative skills they have.* We know how to evaluate as human beings, just as we already know how to speak, and we can improve both by education, practice, and reflection. In addition to strengthening evaluation as an institution, we should augment our personal skills as well.

20. *Reflectivity is a critical thinking process.* Reflectivity is a set of epistemic values and skills. These include collecting information before making up one's mind, seeking diverse opinions before coming to conclusions, thinking deliberately about problems before responding, calibrating opinion to degrees of evidence, thinking about future consequences, and weighing pluses and minuses.

21. *Framing situations and events is a central strategy for understanding; reframing is a key strategy for change.* Moral feelings are attached to frames, to descriptions of reality rather than to reality itself. Preferences are about framed problems, and moral intuitions are about descriptions. Some frames are better than others in thinking about problems (Kahneman, 2011, 370–371).

22. *Evaluating can mean perceiving and acting on several frameworks simultaneously.* Sometimes we need complex ideas to guide practices. These might include considering several frameworks simultaneously. For example, instead of evaluating with only one template in mind, we might evaluate with several frameworks in mind. We might see evaluating as involving the interaction of several communities instead of one. We might understand validity as a complex concept with several dimensions instead of one. We might consider the views of many stakeholders instead of a few.

23. *Cognitive research has provided empirical support for concepts long recognized in the arts and employed in evaluations, such as interpreting events through framing, stories, plots, and metaphors.* We have used story lines, plots, narratives, and other framing devices to construct evaluations. Indeed, textbooks in evaluation rely on metaphoric structures to enhance coherence and understanding. The utility of these devices in thinking has been validated by empirical research. They are elements of understanding, not simply embellishments.

24. *Practical wisdom, what evaluators learn from experience, is more important in how evaluation studies are conducted than generally recognized.* Practical wisdom, along with theory and context, determine much of what we do in evaluations. We may not fully recognize the influence of practical knowledge or strive to improve it.

25. *Practical wisdom is acquired primarily from direct experience, but might be enhanced vicariously.* Although our learning of practical wisdom comes from what we infer from experience, we can enhance this knowledge by absorbing vicarious experiences, such as those presented in case studies and evaluation fiction.

References

Astbury, B. (2013). Some reflections on Pawson's *Science of Evaluation: A realist manifesto. Evaluation, 19*(4), 381–401.

Berliner, D. C., Glass, G. V., & Associates. (2014). *50 myths and lies that threaten America's public schools: The real crisis in education.* New York: Teachers College Press.

Bhaskar, R. (1979). *The possibility of naturalism.* Atlantic Highlands, NJ: Humanities Press.

Buffett. W. (2009). *Annual report of Berkshire Hathaway.* Omaha, Nebraska.

Campbell, D. T., & Stanley, J. (1966). *Experimental and quasi-experimental design for research.* Chicago, IL: Rand McNally.

Carnap, R. (1934). *The unity of science.* London, UK: Kegan, Paul, Trench, Hubner.

Cronbach, L. J. (1982). *Designing evaluations of educational and social programs.* San Francisco, CA: Jossey-Bass.

Davidson, D. (2001). *Subjective, intersubjective, objective.* Oxford, UK: Clarendon Press.

Davidson, D. (2004). *Problems of rationality.* Oxford, UK: Oxford University Press.

Dewey. J. (1927). *The public and its problems.* University Park, PA: Pennsylvania State University Press.

Dryzek, J. S. (2000). *Deliberative democracy and beyond.* Oxford, UK: Oxford University Press.

Dunne, J. (1993). *Back to the rough ground.* Notre Dame, IN: University of Notre Dame Press.

Elster, J. (Ed.). (1998). *Deliberative democracy.* Cambridge, UK: Cambridge University Press.

Fishkin, J. S. (1991). *Democracy and deliberation.* New Haven, CN: Yale University Press.

Evaluating, pages 133–138

Giddens, A. (1984). *The constitution of society*. Berkeley, CA: University of California Press.

Gilens, M. (2012). *Affluence and influence*. Princeton, NJ: Princeton University Press.

Glass, G. V. (2008). *Fertilizers, pills, and magnetic strips: The fate of public education in America*. Charlotte NC: Information Age Publishing.

Greene, J. (2003). War and peace . . . and evaluation. In O. Karlsson (Ed.), *Studies in educational policy and educational philosophy, 2*. Sweden: Uppsala University (www.upi.artisan.se).

Greene, J. (2005). Various entries. S. M. Mathison (Ed.), *Encyclopedia of evaluation*. Sage: Thousand Oaks, CA.

Greene, J. C. (1997). Evaluation as advocacy. *Evaluation Practice, 18*, 25–35.

Greene, J. C. (2000). Challenges in practicing deliberative democratic evaluation. In K. E. Ryan & L. DeStefano (Eds.), *Evaluation as a democratic process: Promoting inclusion, dialogue and deliberation*. New Directions for Evaluation, No. 85 (pp. 13–26). San Francisco, CA: Jossey-Bass.

Greene, J. C. (2013). Making the world a better place through evaluation. In M. C. Alkin (Ed.), *Evaluation roots* (pp. 208–217). Newbury Park, CA: SAGE.

Gutmann, A. & Thompson, D. (1996). *Democracy and disagreement*. Cambridge, MA: Belknap Press.

Gutmann, A., & Thompson, D. (2004). *Why deliberative democracy?* Princeton, NJ: Princeton University Press.

Hanberger, A. (2001). Policy and program evaluation, civil society, and democracy. *American Journal of Evaluation, 22*(2), 211–228.

Harre, R. (2009). Saving critical realism. *Journal for the Theory of Social Behaviour, 39*(2), 129–143.

Haug, P. (1996). Evaluation of government reforms. *Evaluation, 2*, 417–430.

Henry, G. T. (2000). Benefits and limitations of deliberation. In K. E. Ryan & L. DeStefano (Eds.), *Evaluation as a democratic process: Promoting inclusion, dialogue and deliberation*. New Directions for Evaluation, No. 85 (pp. 91–96). San Francisco, CA: Jossey-Bass.

Hood, S. Hopson, R., & Frierson, H. (Eds.). (2005). *The role of culture and cultural context*. Charlotte, NC: Information Age Publishing.

House, E. R. (1980). *Evaluating with validity*. Beverly Hills, CA: SAGE.

House, E. R. (1983). How we think about evaluation. In E. R. House (Ed.), *Philosophy of evaluation*. New Directions for Program Evaluation, No. 19 (pp. 5–25). San Francisco, CA: Jossey Bass.

House, E. R. (1991). Realism in research. *Educational Researcher, 20*(6), 2–9 and 25.

House, E. R. (1993). *Professional evaluation*. Newbury Park, CA: SAGE.

House, E. R. (2001). Unfinished business: Causes and values. *American Journal of Evaluation, 22*(3), 309–315.

House, E. R. (2007). *Regression to the mean: A novel of evaluation politics*. Charlotte, NC: Information Age Publishing.

House, E. R. (2011). Conflict of interest and Campbellian validity. *New Directions for Evaluation, 2011*(130), 69–80.

House, E. R. (2011, June 3). Decision making in evaluation: What's Marv's opinion worth? Symposium in honor of Marvin Alkin. UCLA, Los Angeles, CA.

House, E. R. (2012). Work memoir. In M. C. Alkin (Ed.), *Evaluation roots* (2nd ed., pp. 198–207). Thousand Oaks, CA: SAGE.

House, E. R. (2013). Evaluation's conflicted future. In S. I. Donaldson (Ed.), *The future of evaluation in society* (pp. 63–72). Charlotte, NC: Information Publications.

House, E. R., & Howe, K. R. (1999). *Values in evaluation and social research.* Thousand Oaks, CA: SAGE.

House, E. R., & Howe, K. R. (2000). Deliberative democratic evaluation. In K. E. Ryan & L. DeStefano (Eds.), *Evaluation as a democratic process: Promoting inclusion, dialogue and deliberation* (pp. 3–12). (New Directions for Evaluation, No. 85). San Francisco, CA: Jossey-Bass.

House, E. R. (2012). Democratizing qualitative research. In S. D. Lapan, M. T. Quartaroli, & F. J. Riemer (Eds.), *Qualitative research* (pp. 451–472). San Francisco, CA: Jossey-Bass.

Howe, K., & Ashcraft, C. (2005). Deliberative democratic evaluation: Successes and limitations of an evaluation of school choice. *Teachers College Record, 107*(10), 2275–2298.

Hume, D. (1739/1978). *A treatise of human nature.* Oxford, UK: Oxford University Press. (Original work published 1739.).

Julnes. G. (Ed.). (2012). *Promoting valuation in the public interest: Informing policies for judging value in evaluation.* New Directions for Evaluation, No. 133. San Francisco, CA: Jossey-Bass.

Kahneman, D. (2011). *Thinking, fast and slow.* New York: Farrar, Strauss, and Giroux.

Karlsson, O. (1996). A critical dialogue in evaluation: How can interaction between evaluation and politics be tackled? *Evaluation,* (2), 405–416.

Karlsson, O. (2003). Evaluation politics in Europe: Trends and tendencies. In O. Karlsson (Ed.), *Studies in educational policy and educational philosophy, 1.* Sweden: Uppsala University (www.upi.artisan.se).

Karlsson Vestman O., & Segerholm, C. (2009). Dialogue, deliberation, and democracy in educational evaluation. In K. E. Ryan & J. B. Cousins (Eds.), *The international handbook of educational evaluation* (pp. 465–485). London: Sage Publications.

King, J. A. (1998). Making sense of participatory evaluation. In E. Whitmore (Ed.), *Understanding and practicing participatory evaluation.* New Directions in Evaluation, No. 80 (pp. 57–67). San Francisco, CA: Jossey-Bass,

Koestler, A. (1964). *The act of creation.* New York: McMillan.

Krogstrup, H. K. (2003). User participation in evaluation—Top down and bottom-up perspectives. In O. Karlsson (Ed.). *Studies in educational policy and educational philosophy. No 1.* Sweden: Uppsala University (www.upi.artisan.se)

Kushner, S. (2000). *Personalizing evaluation.* London: SAGE.

Lovibond, S. (1983). *Realism and imagination in ethics.* Minneapolis: University of Minnesota Press.

MacDonald, B. (1977). A political classification of evaluation studies. In D. Hamilton (Ed.), *Beyond the numbers game* (pp. 224–227). London, UK: MacMillan.

MacDonald, B., & Kushner, S. (2004). Democratic evaluation. In S. Mathison (Ed.), *Encyclopedia of evaluation* (pp. 109–113). Thousand Oaks, CA: SAGE.

Mackie, J. L. (1977). *Ethics: Inventing right and wrong.* Harmondsworth, UK: Penguin.

Mark, M. M., Donaldson, S. I., & Campbell, B. (Eds.) (2011). *Social psychology and evaluation.* New York: Guilford Press.

Mark, M. M., Henry, G. T., & Julnes, G. (2000). *Evaluation.* San Francisco, CA: Jossey-Bass.

Mathison, S. (2000). Deliberation, evaluation and democracy. In K. E. Ryan & L. DeStefano (Eds.), *Evaluation as a democratic process: Promoting inclusion, dialogue and deliberation.* New Directions for Evaluation, No. 85 (pp. 85–89). San Francisco, CA: Jossey-Bass.

Meehl, P. E. (1954). *Clinical versus statistical prediction.* Minneapolis: University of Minnesota Press.

Michotte, A. (1963). *The perception of causality.* Andover, MA: Methuen.

Mohr, L. B. (1999). The qualitative method of impact analysis. *American Journal of Evaluation, 20*(1), 69–84.

Morris, M. (2011). The good, the bad, and the evaluator: 25 years of AJE ethics. *American Journal of Evaluation, 32*(1), 134–151.

Murray, R. (2002). Citizens' control of evaluations. *Evaluation, 8*(1), 81–100.

Norris, N. (1990). *Understanding educational evaluation.* New York: St. Martin's Press.

Patton, M. Q. (2002). A vision of evaluation that strengthens democracy. *Evaluation, 8*(1) 125–139.

Pawson, R., & Tilley, N. (1997). *Realistic evaluation.* London: SAGE.

Pearson, K. (1911). *The grammar of science.* New York, NY: Meridian Books. Reprinted in 1957.

Putnam, H. (2002). *The collapse of the fact/value dichotomy.* Cambridge, MA: Harvard.

Putnam. H. (2004). *Ethics without ontology.* Cambridge, MA: Harvard University Press.

Quine, W. V. (1962). *From a logical point of view* (2nd ed.). Cambridge, MA: Harvard.

Rawls, J. (1961). *A theory of justice.* Cambridge, MA: Harvard University Press.

Ross, D. (1991). *The origins of American social science.* Cambridge, UK: University of Cambridge Press.

Rossi, P. H., Freeman, H. E., & Wright, S. R. (1979). *Evaluation: A systematic approach.* Beverly Hills, CA: SAGE.

Ryan, K. E., & DeStefano, L. (Eds.). (2000). *Evaluation as a democratic process: Promoting inclusion, dialogue and deliberation.* New Directions for Evaluation, No. 85. San Francisco, CA: Jossey-Bass.

Sanna, L. J., Panter, A. T., Cohen, T. R., & Kennedy, L. A. (2011). Planning the future and assessing the past. In M. M. Mark, S. I. Donaldson, & B. Campbell (Eds.), *Social psychology and evaluation* (pp. 166–186). New York: Guilford Press.

Scheffler, I. (1967). *Science and subjectivity.* Indianapolis, IN: Bobbs-Merrill.

Schwandt, T. A. (2003). In O. Karlsson (Ed.). *Studies in educational policy and educational philosophy 2.* Sweden: Uppsala University (www.upi.artisan.se).

Schwandt, T. A. (2005). The centrality of practice to evaluation. *American Journal of Evaluation, 26*(1), 95–105.

Schwandt, T. A. (2008). Educating for intelligent belief in evaluation. *American Journal of Evaluation. 29*(2), 139–150.

Schwartz, B., & Sharpe, K. (2010). *Practical wisdom.* New York: Riverside Books.

Scriven, M. (1980). *The logic of evaluation.* Inverness, CA: Edgepress.

Scriven, M. (1969). Logical positivism and the behavioral sciences. In P. Achenstein & S. Barker (Eds.), *The legacy of logical positivism* (pp. 195–210). Baltimore, MD: John Hopkins University Press.

Scriven, M. (1972). Objectivity and subjectivity in educational research. In L. G. Thomas (Ed.), *Philosophical redirection of educational research* (pp. 94–142). Chicago, IL: National Society for the Study of Education.

Scriven, M. (1973). Goal-free evaluation. In E. R. House (Ed.), *School evaluation* (pp. 319–328). Berkeley, CA: McCutcheon.

Scriven, M. (2012). The logic of valuing. In G. Julnes (Ed.), *Promoting valuation in the public interest: Informing policies for judging value in evaluation.* New Directions for Evaluation, No. 133 (pp. 17–28). San Francisco, CA: Jossey-Bass.

Scriven, M. (2013). The foundation and future of evaluation. In S. I. Donaldson (Ed.), *The future of evaluation in society* (pp. 11–44). Charlotte, NC: Information Age Publishing.

Segerholm, C. (2003). To govern in silence: An essay on the political in national evaluations of the public schools in Sweden. In O. Karlsson (Ed.), *Studies in educational policy and educational philosophy, 2.* Sweden: Uppsala University (www.upi.artisan.se).

Shiller, R. (2000). *Irrational exuberance.* Princeton, NJ: Princeton University Press.

Simons, H. (1987). *Getting to know schools in a democracy.* London: Falmer Press.

Stake, R. E. (1967). The countenance of educational evaluation. *Teachers College Press, 68,* 523–540.

Stake, R. E. (1978). The case study method in social inquiry, *Educational Researcher 7,* 5–8.

Stake, R. E., Migotsky, C., Davis, R., Cisneros, E., DePaul, G., Dunbar, C., ... Chaves, I., (1997). The evolving syntheses of program value, *Evaluation Practice, 18,* 2, 89–103.

Stanovich, K. E. (2009). *What intelligent tests miss.* New Haven and London: Yale University Press.

Stanovich, K. E. (2011). *Rationality and the reflective mind.* New York: Oxford University Press.

Stein, J. G. (2001). *The cult of efficiency.* Toronto: Anansi.

Suskind, R. (2011). *Confidence men: Wall Street, Washington, and the education of a president.* New York: Harper Collins.

Taylor, C. (1975). *Hegel.* Cambridge, UK: Cambridge University Press.

Toulmin, S. (2001) *Return to reason.* Cambridge, MA: Harvard University Press.

Vygotsky, L. S. (1978). *Mind in society.* Cambridge, MA: Harvard University Press.

72110036R00088

Made in the USA
Middletown, DE
03 May 2018